W9-AAG-874

*GUIDE TO*

# SQL

*The
Standard
Relational
Database
Language*

Microsoft
P R E S S

PUBLISHED BY
Microsoft Press
A Division of Microsoft Corporation
16011 NE 36th Way, Box 97017, Redmond, Washington 98073-9717

Library of Congress Cataloging in Publication Data

Viescas, John, 1947-
Quick reference guide to SQL.
1. SQL (Computer program language)   2. Data base management.
I. Title.
QA76.73.S67V54      1989      005.75'6   89-2525
ISBN 1-55615-198-5

Printed and bound in the United States of America.

1 2 3 4 5 6 7 8 9 WAKWAK 3 2 1 0 9

Distributed to the book trade in the United States by Harper & Row.

Distributed to the book trade in Canada by General Publishing
Company, Ltd.

Distributed to the book trade outside the United States and Canada
by Penguin Books Ltd.

Penguin Books Ltd., Harmondsworth, Middlesex, England
Penguin Books Australia Ltd., Ringwood, Victoria, Australia
Penguin Books N.Z. Ltd., 182-190 Wairau Road, Auckland 10,
New Zealand

British Cataloging in Publication Data available


Project Editor: Nancy Siadek
Technical Editor: Mary Ottaway

# *Contents*

## Data Definition Language

## Data Control Language

## Appendixes

# Introduction

This quick reference is a guide to industry-standard SQL (Structured Query Language). It includes base ANSI-86 SQL and all common extensions found in the major commercial implementations.

SQL is usually divided into three major components: Data Manipulation Language (DML), Data Control Language (DCL), and Data Definition Language (DDL). This quick reference contains a section on each component and an appendix that describes common data types, arithmetic operators, and reserved words. Within each section, SQL statements, major clauses, and subfunctions are arranged alphabetically.

**Data Manipulation Language:** Contains the language components and concepts for manipulating information stored in tables. This guide includes forms of the DELETE, INSERT, SELECT, and UPDATE statements that you can issue directly from an interactive, or direct, terminal interface. It also includes language constructs for embedding SQL data manipulation commands in an application language such as COBOL or C. In addition, common forms of dynamic DML that are being considered for inclusion in the ANSI standard and that are found in many implementations of the language are documented here. Dynamic DML statements are SQL statements that are defined during a program's runtime and that usually vary among executions of the program. Note that because dynamic DML is not yet standardized, statements might vary greatly among implementations.

**Data Definition Language:** Includes the most common syntax you use to define, alter, or delete the tables in which you store data.

Caution: This portion of the language is most likely to be different among implementations. Refer to your product documentation when attempting to do more than basic table definition or deletion.

**Data Control Language:** Contains elements that are useful if you are working in a multiuser environment in which locking information, securing tables, or establishing transaction boundaries is important.

In this guide, noninteractive SQL examples consist of statements embedded in segments of application programs written in COBOL or C. SQL is itself a sub-language and varies little as used within different application languages.

# References

| Source | Document Number | Title |
|---|---|---|
| ANSI | X3.135-1986 | *Database Language SQL* and Annexes A through F |
| IBM | SC26-4346-0 | *IBM Database 2 SQL Reference* (Version 1, Release 3) |
| Microsoft | 510880018-100-O00-0988 | *SQL Server Language Reference* |
| Oracle | 3203-V2.0 | *SQL\*Plus Reference Guide* |
| Tandem | 84258 | *NonStop SQL Programming Reference Manual* |

## Syntax Conventions

The following conventions describe the SQL syntax you will encounter in this quick reference guide.

| Convention | Meaning |
|---|---|
| UPPERCASE | Uppercase letters indicate keywords and reserved words that you must enter exactly as shown. Note that some implementations of SQL (particularly interactive ones) allow you to enter lowercase keywords. |
| *italic* | Italicized words represent variables you supply. |
| Brackets [ ] | Brackets enclose optional items, separated by a pipe ( ¦ ) if more than one item is listed. Choose one or none of the elements. Do not enter the brackets or the pipe. |
| Braces { } | Braces enclose one or more options, separated by a pipe ( ¦ ) if more than one is listed. Choose one item from the list. Do not enter the braces or the pipe. |
| Ellipses ,... | Ellipses indicate that you can repeat an item one or more times. When a comma is shown with ellipses, enter the comma between items. |

**Notes:** You must enter all other symbols, such as parentheses and colons, exactly as they appear in the syntax line.

Most implementations allow you to continue a statement across multiple input lines but require that you enter a semicolon to indicate the end of the statement.

COBOL keywords and variables in this guide appear in uppercase letters. C keywords and variables appear in lowercase letters.

# Data Manipulation Language

## BEGIN DECLARE SECTION Statement

### Syntax:

BEGIN DECLARE SECTION

### Description:

Denotes the beginning of a section in which variables are declared in the host language. These variables are used in subsequent SQL statements within a program.

### Notes:

- Only use this statement embedded in an application program. You must precede this statement with the EXEC SQL statement prefix and follow it with the SQL statement terminator appropriate to the application language. (See END-EXEC Statement Terminator.)

- Within a COBOL program, you can use this statement only in the working storage section. Other languages permit the use of this statement anywhere in the program.

- You must use an END DECLARE SECTION statement to terminate the host-variable declare section. No executable statements can be placed within the variable declare portion of the program.

- You can create more than one host-variable declare section within a program.

- Generally, the variables contained within a declare section must be simple variables (not compound structures), must contain no redefines, and must not define arrays. (The character array used in C for manipulating strings is an exception to this rule.)

- In most implementations, you cannot include an SQLCA or SQLDA within the declare section.

- Some implementations do not require the BEGIN DECLARE SECTION and END DECLARE SECTION statements. Refer to your product documentation for details.

## Examples:

In a COBOL program, to declare a variable *ZIP-CODE* for use within a WHERE clause in a SELECT statement, enter the following:

```
WORKING-STORAGE SECTION.
⋮
EXEC SQL
BEGIN DECLARE SECTION END-EXEC.
01  ZIP-CODE    PIC 9(5).
EXEC SQL
END DECLARE SECTION END-EXEC.
```

In a C program, to declare a similar variable *zip_code*, enter the following:

```
EXEC SQL
BEGIN DECLARE SECTION;
char *zip_code;
EXEC SQL
END DECLARE SECTION;
```

## See Also:

END DECLARE SECTION Statement and INCLUDE Directive.

---

# CLOSE Statement

## Syntax:

CLOSE *cursor-name*

## Description:

Closes an open cursor (a pointer to a logical table). You define a cursor in a DECLARE CURSOR statement and open the defined cursor with an OPEN statement. If you did not previously open a particular cursor, your program receives an error when you attempt to close that cursor.

## Notes:

■ Only use this statement embedded in an application program. You must precede this statement with the EXEC SQL statement prefix and follow it with the SQL statement terminator appropriate to the application language. (See END-EXEC Statement Terminator.)

- When you close a cursor, the logical table that was created when you opened that cursor is usually destroyed.

- Execution of a COMMIT WORK statement closes all cursors.

## Examples:

In a COBOL program, to close a cursor named NEWCUST, enter the following:

```
EXEC SQL
CLOSE NEWCUST END-EXEC.
```

In a C program, to close a cursor named ACMEOWE, enter the following:

```
EXEC SQL
CLOSE ACMEOWE;
```

## See Also:

COMMIT Data Control Statement (Data Definition Language), DECLARE CURSOR Statement, END-EXEC Statement Terminator, EXEC SQL Statement Prefix, FETCH Statement, and OPEN Statement.

# DECLARE CURSOR Statement

## Syntax:

DECLARE *cursor-name* CURSOR FOR
  *select-statement* [{UNION ¦ UNION ALL} *select-statement*]...
  [[FOR UPDATE OF {*column-name*},...] ¦
  [ORDER BY {{*column-name* ¦ *integer*} [ASC ¦ DESC]},...]]

## Description:

Declares a cursor (a pointer to a logical table) to be processed in an application program. The *select-statement*, along with the optional UNION with one or more additional *select-statements*, defines the logical table processed by this cursor.

## Notes:

- Only use this statement embedded in an application program. You must precede this statement with the EXEC SQL statement prefix and follow it with the SQL statement terminator appropriate to the application language. (See END-EXEC Statement Terminator.)

- To update the logical table associated with this cursor, you must include a FOR UPDATE clause that specifies the columns that are eligible to be updated.

- To specify an order for the rows presented to your application program through this cursor, you must include an ORDER BY clause specifying the column(s) that contains the particular values that will determine the row order. You can identify the column(s) by specifying the column name(s) or relative column number(s). (1 is the first column.)

- Be aware that a *column-name* can be ambiguous because the same name might appear more than once in a *select-list* of a SELECT statement, or different column names might appear in the same position because of a UNION operation. If the column name is ambiguous, you must use a relative column number in the ORDER BY clause.

- You can specify multiple columns in the ORDER BY clause and also specify ascending (ASC) or descending (DESC) ordering for each column. Some implementations might not allow the use of both ASC and DESC in the ORDER BY list. If you specify neither ASC nor DESC, ASC is assumed. To specify more than one column, separate the column names or numbers with a comma. Note that you can use a combination of names and numbers in the clause.

- You cannot update the logical table associated with a cursor declared with an ORDER BY clause.

- You cannot update the logical table associated with a cursor declared with a UNION operation.

- You cannot update the logical table associated with a cursor declared with a SELECT statement that includes a column function (AVG, MAX, or MIN), the DISTINCT keyword, the GROUP BY or HAVING clauses, or a subSELECT clause that references the same base table as the SELECT statement.

- You cannot update the logical table associated with a cursor declared with a SELECT statement that references more than one table or that references a read-only view in the FROM clause.

- Some implementations support the INTERSECT or MINUS query operator in addition to UNION. Refer to your product documentation for specific details.

## Examples:

In a COBOL program, to declare a cursor that includes only customers who first did business in 1988 and that lists them in ascending order by zip code, enter the following:

```
EXEC SQL
DECLARE NEWCUST CURSOR FOR
  SELECT CUSTNAME, ADDRESS
    FROM CUSTOMER
    WHERE FIRSDATE = '1988'
    ORDER BY ZIP ASC END-EXEC.
```

In a C program, to declare a cursor that includes all payments owed to the Acme Mail Order Company and that allows the check number to be updated, enter the following:

```
EXEC SQL
DECLARE ACMEOWE CURSOR FOR
  SELECT PAYEENAME, ADDRESS, AMTOWED, CHECKNUM
    FROM ACCTSPAY
    WHERE PAYEENAME = 'Acme Mail Order Company'
    FOR UPDATE OF CHECKNUM;
```

### See Also:

CLOSE Statement, DELETE...WHERE CURRENT OF Statement, END-EXEC Statement Terminator, EXEC SQL Statement Prefix, FETCH Statement, INTERSECT Query Operator, MINUS Query Operator, OPEN Statement, ORDER BY Clause, SELECT Statement, subSELECT Clause, UNION Query Operator, and UPDATE...WHERE CURRENT OF Statement.

# DECLARE CURSOR Statement (Dynamic SQL)

## Syntax:

DECLARE *cursor-name* CURSOR FOR *statement-name*

## Description:

Dynamically declares a cursor (a pointer to a logical table) to be used in an application program. The *statement-name* refers to the name that you defined in a previous preparation of the SELECT statement that defines the logical table.

## Notes:

■ Only use this statement embedded in an application program. You must precede this statement with the EXEC SQL statement prefix and follow it with the SQL statement terminator appropriate to the application language. (See END-EXEC Statement Terminator.)

■ You can include parameter indicators in the prepared SELECT statement. The examples in this guide use the question mark (?) as the
parameter indicator. Some implementations might use a different
character; refer to your product documentation for details. You must
provide values for the parameter indicators in the subsequent OPEN
statement.

■ To update the logical table associated with this cursor, you must
have included a FOR UPDATE OF clause in the SELECT statement
referred to by *statement-name*.

■ You cannot update the logical table associated with a cursor
declared with an ORDER BY clause.

■ You cannot update the logical table associated with a cursor
declared with a UNION operation.

■ You cannot update the logical table associated with a cursor
declared with a SELECT statement that includes a column function
(AVG, COUNT, MAX, MIN, or SUM), the DISTINCT keyword, the
GROUP BY or HAVING clauses, or a subSELECT clause that references the same base table as the given SELECT statement.

■ You cannot update the logical table associated with a cursor that
was declared using a SELECT statement that references more than
one table or that references a read-only view in the FROM clause.

## Examples:

In a COBOL program, to dynamically declare a cursor that includes
only customers who first did business in 1988 (the date provided as a
parameter to an OPEN statement) and that lists them in ascending
order by zip code, enter the following:

```
WORKING-STORAGE SECTION.
  ⋮
EXEC SQL
BEGIN DECLARE SECTION END-EXEC.
 01  DYNAMIC-STATEMENT    PIC X(250) VALUE
 -     'SELECT CUSTNAME, ADDRESS
 -       'FROM CUSTOMER
 -       'WHERE FIRSTDATE = ?
 -       'ORDER BY ZIP ASC'.
 01  SELECT-DATE          PIC 9999.
EXEC SQL
END DECLARE SECTION END-EXEC.
  ⋮
```

```
PROCEDURE DIVISION.
    ⋮
    EXEC SQL
    PREPARE CUST-SEARCH FROM :DYNAMIC-STATEMENT END-EXEC.
    ⋮
    EXEC SQL
    DECLARE NEWCUST CURSOR FOR CUST-SEARCH END-EXEC.
    ⋮
    MOVE '1988' TO SELECT-DATE.
    EXEC SQL
    OPEN NEWCUST USING :SELECT-DATE END-EXEC.
```

In a C program, to dynamically declare a cursor that includes all payments owed to the Acme Mail Order Company and that allows the check number to be inserted, enter the following:

```
EXEC SQL
BEGIN DECLARE SECTION;
    char *dynam_select =
      "SELECT PAYEENAME, ADDRESS, AMTOWED, CHECKNUM \
        FROM ACCTSPAY \
        WHERE PAYEENAME = 'Acme Mail Order Company' \
        FOR UPDATE OF CHECKNUM";
EXEC SQL
END DECLARE SECTION;
⋮
EXEC SQL
PREPARE UPDATACCT FROM :dynam_select;
⋮
EXEC SQL
DECLARE ACMEOWE CURSOR FOR UPDATACCT;
⋮
EXEC SQL
OPEN ACMEOWE USING;
```

## See Also:

CLOSE Statement, DELETE...WHERE CURRENT OF Statement, END-EXEC Statement Terminator, EXEC SQL Statement Prefix, FETCH Statement (Dynamic SQL), INTERSECT Query Operator, MINUS Query Operator, OPEN Statement (Dynamic SQL), PREPARE Statement, SELECT Statement, subSELECT Clause, UNION Query Operator, and UPDATE...WHERE CURRENT OF Statement.

# DELETE Statement

## Syntax:

DELETE FROM {*table-name* ¦ *view-name*} [*correlation-name*]
  [WHERE *search-condition*]

## Description:

Deletes one or more rows from a table or view. The WHERE clause is
optional. If you do not specify a WHERE clause, all rows are deleted
from the table or view that you specify in the FROM clause. If you
specify a WHERE clause, the *search-condition* is applied to each row
in the table or view, and only those rows that evaluate to true are
deleted.

## Notes:

- You can embed this statement in an application program if you precede it with the required EXEC SQL statement prefix and follow it
  with the SQL statement terminator appropriate to the application
  language. (See END-EXEC Statement Terminator.)

- Some SQL implementations support only a *table-name* in the FROM
  clause. Generally, when a *view-name* is supported in the FROM
  clause, the view must be constructed from only one base table.

- If you specify a *view-name* in a DELETE statement, the view must
  reference a single base table, must not contain an ORDER BY
  clause, and must not be constructed using the UNION, INTERSECT,
  or MINUS query operators. The view also must not contain a column function (AVG, COUNT, MAX, MIN, or SUM), the DISTINCT
  keyword, the GROUP BY or HAVING clauses, or a subSELECT
  clause that references the same base table as the DELETE statement.

- You can optionally supply a *correlation-name* for each table or view
  name. You can use this *correlation-name* as an alias for the full
  table name when qualifying column names in the WHERE clause
  and subclauses. You must use a *correlation-name* when referring to
  a *column-name* that occurs in more than one table in the FROM
  clause.

- If you specify a *search-condition*, you can reference only columns
  found in the target table or view. If you use a subquery in the
  *search-condition*, you must not reference the target table or the view
  or any underlying table of the view in the subquery.

## Examples:

To delete all rows in the ACCTSPAY table, enter the following:

```
DELETE FROM ACCTSPAY;
```

To delete all rows in the ACCTSPAY table that are from Acme Mail Order Company, enter the following:

```
DELETE FROM ACCTSPAY
  WHERE PAYEENAME = 'Acme Mail Order Company';
```

## See Also:

INSERT Statement, Search-condition, subSELECT Clause, and Predicates.

---

# DELETE...WHERE CURRENT OF Statement

## Syntax:

DELETE FROM {*table-name* ¦ *view-name*}
  WHERE CURRENT OF *cursor-name*

## Description:

Deletes the row of the table or view on which the cursor specified by *cursor-name* is positioned. The related DECLARE CURSOR statement must appear before this statement within an application program. Also, the cursor must be opened with the OPEN statement and positioned on a row via a FETCH statement. If the deletion is successful, the cursor is positioned before the next row of the result table. If the row deleted is the last row, the cursor is positioned after the last row.

## Notes:

■ Only use this statement embedded in an application program. You must precede this statement with the EXEC SQL statement prefix and follow it with the SQL statement terminator appropriate to the application language. (See END-EXEC Statement Terminator.)

■ Some SQL implementations support only a *table-name* in the FROM clause. Generally, when a *view-name* is supported in the FROM clause, the view must be constructed from only one base table.

- The *table-name* or *view-name* specified must be the same as that used in the SELECT clause of the DECLARE CURSOR statement. In addition, it must be possible to update the result table of the DECLARE CURSOR statement. Refer to the section on DECLARE CURSOR for rules about updatable cursors.

## Examples:

In a COBOL program, to delete the row pointed to by a cursor named BADCUST that was declared as a selection on the table CUSTOMER, enter the following:

```
EXEC SQL
DELETE FROM CUSTOMER
  WHERE CURRENT OF BADCUST END-EXEC.
```

In a C program, to delete the row pointed to by a cursor named ACMEOWE that was declared as a selection on the table ACCTSPAY, enter the following:

```
EXEC SQL
DELETE FROM ACCTSPAY
  WHERE CURRENT OF ACMEOWE;
```

## See Also:

DECLARE CURSOR Statement, END-EXEC Statement Terminator, EXEC SQL Statement Prefix, FETCH Statement, INSERT Statement, and OPEN Statement.

# DESCRIBE Statement (Dynamic SQL)

## Syntax:

DESCRIBE *statement-name* INTO *sqlda-name*

## Description:

Returns information about the output variables in a dynamic SELECT statement that has been readied for execution using a PREPARE statement. The information is returned into an SQL descriptor area (SQLDA) that can subsequently be used in a dynamic EXECUTE, FETCH, or OPEN statement. The DESCRIBE statement can be used to pass variables retrieved from the SQL system from one statement to another without needing to know the attributes of the variables in advance.

## Notes:

■ Only use this statement embedded in an application program. You must precede this statement with the EXEC SQL statement prefix and follow it with the SQL statement terminator appropriate to the application language. (See END-EXEC Statement Terminator.)

■ Format of the SQLDA varies depending on the specific SQL implementation. Many products support definition of the SQLDA via an INCLUDE directive. Refer to your product documentation for details.

## Examples:

In a COBOL program, to obtain the descriptive information for variables returned by a dynamically declared cursor named CUST-SEARCH, enter the following:

```
WORKING-STORAGE SECTION.
 ⋮
EXEC SQL
INCLUDE SQLDA END-EXEC.
 ⋮
EXEC SQL
BEGIN DECLARE SECTION END-EXEC.
 01  DYNAMIC-STATEMENT     PIC X(250) VALUE
 -      'SELECT CUSTNAME, ADDRESS
 -        'FROM CUSTOMER
 -        'WHERE FIRSTDATE = ?
 -        'ORDER BY ZIP ASC'.
 01  SELECT-DATE           PIC 9999.
EXEC SQL
END DECLARE SECTION END-EXEC.
 ⋮
PROCEDURE DIVISION.
    ⋮
    EXEC SQL
    PREPARE CUST-SEARCH FROM :DYNAMIC-STATEMENT END-EXEC.
    ⋮
    EXEC SQL
    DESCRIBE CUST-SEARCH INTO :SQLDA END-EXEC.
```

**Note:** The statement INCLUDE SQLDA (used in this example) is not supported for COBOL in every implementation. The example assumes that the INCLUDE directive creates a data structure named SQLDA. Some implementations of the INCLUDE directive allow you to provide a name for the SQLDA structure generated by the INCLUDE directive. See your product documentation for details.

In a C program, to obtain the descriptive information for variables returned by a dynamically declared cursor named CUST_SEARCH, enter the following:

```
EXEC SQL
INCLUDE SQLDA;
  ⋮
EXEC SQL
BEGIN DECLARE SECTION;
char *dynamic_statement =
  "SELECT CUSTNAME, ADDRESS \
     FROM CUSTOMER \
     WHERE FIRSTDATE = ? \
     ORDER BY ZIP ASC";
char *select_date;
EXEC SQL
END DECLARE SECTION;
  ⋮
EXEC SQL
PREPARE CUST_SEARCH FROM :dynamic_statement;
  ⋮
EXEC SQL
DESCRIBE CUST_SEARCH INTO :SQLDA;
```

## See Also:

CLOSE Statement, DECLARE CURSOR Statement (Dynamic SQL), EXECUTE Statement (Dynamic SQL), FETCH Statement (Dynamic SQL), INCLUDE Directive, OPEN Statement (Dynamic SQL), and PREPARE Statement (Dynamic SQL).

# END DECLARE SECTION Statement

## Syntax:

END DECLARE SECTION

## Description:

Denotes the end of the section in which variables are declared in the host language. These variables are used in subsequent embedded SQL statements within a program.

## Notes:

■ Only use this statement embedded in an application program. You must precede this statement with the EXEC SQL statement prefix and follow it with the SQL statement terminator appropriate to the application language. (See END-EXEC Statement Terminator.)

■ Within a COBOL program, you can use this statement only in the working storage section. Other languages permit the use of this statement anywhere in the program.

■ You must code a preceding BEGIN DECLARE SECTION statement in order to begin the host-variable declare section. Executable statements cannot be placed within the variable declaration portion of the program.

■ You can code more than one host-variable declare section within a program.

■ Generally, the variables contained within a declare section must be simple variables (not compound structures), must contain no redefines, and must not define arrays. (The character array used in C for manipulating strings is an exception to this rule.)

■ In most implementations, you cannot include an SQLCA or SQLDA within the declare section.

■ Some implementations do not require you to include the BEGIN DECLARE SECTION and END DECLARE SECTION statements. Refer to your product documentation for details.

## Examples:

In a COBOL program, to declare a variable *ZIP-CODE* that is to be used within the WHERE clause in a SELECT statement, enter the following:

```
WORKING-STORAGE SECTION.
⋮
EXEC SQL
BEGIN DECLARE SECTION END-EXEC.
01  ZIP-CODE     PIC 9(5).
EXEC SQL
END DECLARE SECTION END-EXEC.
```

In a C program, to declare a similar variable *zip_code*, enter the following:

```
EXEC SQL
BEGIN DECLARE SECTION;
char *zip_code;
EXEC SQL
END DECLARE SECTION;
```

## See Also:

BEGIN DECLARE SECTION Statement and INCLUDE Directive.

# END-EXEC Statement Terminator

## Syntax:

END-EXEC[.]

## Description:

Denotes the end of an embedded SQL statement in a COBOL application program. Most languages require a statement terminator. (See the following notes for details.)

## Notes:

- Only use END-EXEC (or the SQL statement terminator appropriate to the language for SQL statements) embedded in an application program.

- A trailing period (.) is required by some COBOL implementations and is generally accepted by all implementations.

- You must use a semicolon (;) instead of END-EXEC as the SQL statement terminator immediately following the last significant character of the SQL statement in the C, Ada, and PL/1 programming languages. Use a semicolon (;) to delimit consecutive SQL statements appearing in a Pascal application program. In COBOL, you can enter the END-EXEC delimiter immediately following the end of the SQL statement or at the beginning of a new line.

- An SQL statement terminator is not required in a Fortran program.

## Examples:

In a COBOL program, to embed a statement that deletes all rows in the ACCTSPAY table, enter the following:

```
EXEC SQL
DELETE FROM ACCTSPAY END-EXEC.
```

In a C, an Ada, or a PL/1 program, to embed a statement that deletes all rows in the ACCTSPAY table, enter the following:

```
EXEC SQL
DELETE FROM ACCTSPAY;
```

## See Also:

EXEC SQL Statement Prefix.

# EXEC SQL Statement Prefix

## Syntax:

EXEC SQL

## Description:

Denotes the beginning of an SQL statement embedded in an application program.

## Notes:

- This statement prefix is required for all SQL statements included in an application program.

- In most implementations, the words *EXEC SQL* must appear together on a single line of the program code. You can enter the enclosed SQL statement immediately following the EXEC SQL delimiter, or you can enter the SQL statement at the beginning of a new line.

## Examples:

In a COBOL program, to embed a statement that deletes all rows in the ACCTSPAY table, enter the following:

```
EXEC SQL
DELETE FROM ACCTSPAY END-EXEC.
```

In a C, an Ada, or a PL/1 program, to embed a statement that deletes all rows in the ACCTSPAY table, enter the following:

```
EXEC SQL
DELETE FROM ACCTSPAY;
```

## See Also:

END-EXEC Statement Terminator.

# EXECUTE Statement (Dynamic SQL)

## Syntax:

EXECUTE *statement-name*
  [USING {:*host-variable*},... ¦
  USING DESCRIPTOR :*host-variable*]

## Description:

Executes the *statement-name* previously defined in a PREPARE statement.

## Notes:

■ Only use this statement embedded in an application program. You must precede this statement with the EXEC SQL statement prefix and follow it with the SQL statement terminator appropriate to the application language. (See END-EXEC Statement Terminator.)

■ The prepared statement cannot be a SELECT statement. Use a cursor to dynamically process a SELECT statement.

■ If the prepared statement contains parameter indicators, you must provide a USING clause to substitute the indicator values before the statement is executed. The examples in this guide use the question mark (?) as the parameter indicator. Some implementations might use a different character. Refer to your product documentation for details.

■ Use the USING :*host-variable* form to provide parameter substitution with variables that are assigned values directly within your program. Use the USING DESCRIPTOR form to point to parameter descriptors. These descriptors are provided for variables in an SQLDA structure that have been assigned values by the SQL system from a previously executed DESCRIBE statement. In either case, the number of variables provided or described must be the same as the number of parameter indicators found in the prepared statement.

## Examples:

In a COBOL program, to dynamically execute an INSERT statement that inserts rows into a table using values dynamically retrieved from another table, enter the following:

```
WORKING-STORAGE SECTION.
    ⋮
EXEC SQL
INCLUDE SQLDA END-EXEC.
    ⋮
EXEC SQL
BEGIN DECLARE SECTION END-EXEC.
01  DYNAMIC-SELECT          PIC X(250) VALUE
-       'SELECT CUSTNAME, ADDRESS
-          'FROM CUSTOMER
-          'WHERE FIRSTDATE = ?
-          'ORDER BY ZIP ASC'.
```

```
01   SELECT-DATE            PIC 9999.
01   DYNAMIC-INSERT         PIC X(150) VALUE
-    'INSERT INTO TEMPCUST VALUES (?,?)'.
 EXEC SQL
 END DECLARE SECTION END-EXEC.
   ⋮
 PROCEDURE DIVISION
     ⋮
*    (prepare the SELECT statement)
     EXEC SQL
     PREPARE CUSTSEARCH FROM :DYNAMIC-SELECT END-EXEC.
     ⋮
*    (describe the SELECT statement output)
     EXEC SQL
     DESCRIBE CUST-SEARCH INTO :SQLDA END-EXEC.
*    (prepare the INSERT statement)
     EXEC SQL
     PREPARE ISRT-CUST FROM :DYNAMIC-INSERT END-EXEC.
     ⋮
*    (declare a cursor on the SELECT statement)
     EXEC SQL
     DECLARE NEWCUST CURSOR FOR CUST-SEARCH END-EXEC.
     ⋮
*    (fetch rows, dynamically execute the INSERT statement)
     MOVE '1988' TO SELECT-DATE.
     EXEC SQL
     OPEN NEWCUST USING :SELECT-DATE END-EXEC.
     EXEC SQL
     WHENEVER NOT FOUND GO TO :DONE END-EXEC.
 LOOP.
     EXEC SQL
     FETCH NEWCUST USING DESCRIPTOR :SQLDA END-EXEC.
     EXEC SQL
     EXECUTE ISRT-CUST USING DESCRIPTOR :SQLDA END-EXEC.
     GO TO LOOP.
 DONE.
     EXEC SQL
     CLOSE NEWCUST END-EXEC.
```

**Note:** The statement INCLUDE SQLDA (used in the example) is not supported for COBOL in every implementation. The example assumes that the INCLUDE directive creates a data structure named SQLDA. Some implementations of the INCLUDE directive allow you to provide a name for the SQLDA structure generated by an INCLUDE directive. See your product documentation for details.

In a C program, to dynamically execute an INSERT statement that inserts rows into a table using values dynamically retrieved from another table (also shown in the COBOL example), enter the following:

```
EXEC SQL
INCLUDE SQLDA;
⋮
EXEC SQL
BEGIN DECLARE SECTION;
char *dynamic_select =
  "SELECT CUSTNAME, ADDRESS \
     FROM CUSTOMER \
     WHERE FIRSTDATE = ? \
     ORDER BY ZIP ASC";
char *select_date;
char *dynamic_insert =
  "INSERT INTO TEMPCUST VALUES (?,?)";
EXEC SQL
END DECLARE SECTION;
⋮
/* prepare the SELECT statement */
EXEC SQL
PREPARE CUST_SEARCH FROM :dynamic_select;
⋮
/* describe the SELECT statement output */
EXEC SQL
DESCRIBE CUST_SEARCH INTO :SQLDA;
/* prepare the INSERT statement */
EXEC SQL
PREPARE ISRT_CUST FROM :dynamic_insert;
⋮
/* declare a cursor on the SELECT statement */
EXEC SQL
DECLARE NEWCUST CURSOR FOR CUST_SEARCH;
⋮
/* fetch rows, dynamically execute the INSERT statement */
select_date = "1988";
EXEC SQL
OPEN NEWCUST USING :select_date;
EXEC SQL
WHENEVER NOT FOUND GO TO :DONE;
for (i =1; i > 0; i++)
   {
   EXEC SQL
   FETCH NEWCUST USING DESCRIPTOR :SQLDA;
   EXEC SQL
   EXECUTE ISRT_CUST USING DESCRIPTOR :SQLDA;
   }
DONE.
EXEC SQL
CLOSE NEWCUST;
```

## See Also:

CLOSE Statement, DECLARE CURSOR Statement (Dynamic SQL), DESCRIBE Statement (Dynamic SQL), FETCH Statement (Dynamic SQL), INCLUDE Directive, INSERT Statement, OPEN Statement (Dynamic SQL), and PREPARE Statement (Dynamic SQL).

# EXECUTE IMMEDIATE Statement (Dynamic SQL)

## Syntax:

EXECUTE IMMEDIATE {:*host-variable* ¦ *string-literal*}

## Description:

Immediately prepares and executes an SQL statement found in a specified *host-variable* or given in a *string-literal*.

## Notes:

■ Only use this statement embedded in an application program. You must precede this statement with the EXEC SQL statement prefix and follow it with the SQL statement terminator appropriate to the application language. (See END-EXEC Statement Terminator.)

■ Some implementations don't allow the use of *string-literal*. Consult your documentation for details.

■ The executed statement cannot be a SELECT statement. Use a cursor to dynamically process a SELECT statement.

■ In most implementations, you cannot immediately execute an OPEN or a CLOSE statement. Some implementations also do not allow the immediate execution of DECLARE CURSOR, DESCRIBE, EXECUTE, FETCH, or PREPARE statements, or INCLUDE or WHENEVER directives. Consult your documentation for details.

■ You cannot include parameter indicators or references to host variables in the immediately executed statement.

## Example:

In a COBOL program, to execute immediately a statement to create a temporary table named TEMPCUST, enter the following:

```
WORKING-STORAGE SECTION.
  ⋮
EXEC SQL
INCLUDE SQLDA END-EXEC.
  ⋮
EXEC SQL
BEGIN DECLARE SECTION END-EXEC.
01  DYNAMIC-CREATE        PIC X(150) VALUE
-    'CREATE TABLE TEMPCUST
-      (CUSTNAME CHAR(30), ADDRESS CHAR(25))'.
EXEC SQL
END DECLARE SECTION END-EXEC.
  ⋮
PROCEDURE DIVISION.
    EXEC SQL
    EXECUTE IMMEDIATE :DYNAMIC-CREATE END-EXEC.
    EXEC SQL
    COMMIT WORK END-EXEC.
```

In a C program, to execute immediately a statement to insert a row into the table called CUSTOMER, enter the following:

```
EXEC SQL
INCLUDE SQLDA;
  ⋮
EXEC SQL
BEGIN DECLARE SECTION;
char *dynamic_insert =
  "INSERT INTO CUSTOMER (CUSTNO, ADDRESS, \
    CITY, STATE, ZIP, FIRSTDATE) \
    VALUES (399, 'Chris Date', 'P.O. Box 1', \
    'San Jose', 'CA', 95000, 881205)";
EXEC SQL
END DECLARE SECTION;
  ⋮
EXEC SQL
EXECUTE IMMEDIATE :dynamic_insert;
EXEC SQL
COMMIT WORK;
```

**Note:** Most implementations require a COMMIT statement to be executed before your program can utilize any change implemented by a Data Definition Language statement issued in the program.

## See Also:

DECLARE CURSOR Statement (Dynamic SQL), FETCH Statement (Dynamic SQL), PREPARE Statement (Dynamic SQL), COMMIT Statement (Data Control Language).

# Expressions

## Syntax:

[+¦-] {*function* ¦ (*expression*) ¦ *literal* ¦ *column-name* ¦
*:host-variable*} [ {+¦-¦*¦/} {*function* ¦ (*expression*) ¦ *literal* ¦
*column-name* ¦ *:host-variable* } ]...

## Description:

Specifies a value in a predicate, in the *select-list* of a SELECT statement or subSELECT clause, or in the SET clause of an UPDATE
statement.

## Notes:

■ *function*—You can specify a column function such as AVG,
COUNT, MAX, MIN, or SUM. Some database systems support additional functions such as STDDEV or VARIANCE. Consult your product documentation for details.

■ (*expression*)—You can construct an expression from multiple expressions separated by operators. See examples on the following
page.

■ *literal*—You can specify a numeric or an alphanumeric constant.
You must enclose an alphanumeric constant in apostrophes. To include an apostrophe in an alphanumeric literal, enter the apostrophe character twice in the literal string. If the expression is
numeric, you must use a numeric constant.

■ *column-name*—You can specify the name of a column in a table or
a view. Generally, you can only use a column name from a table or
view that you have specified in the FROM clause of the statement.
If the expression is an arithmetic expression, you must use a column that contains numeric data.

■ *host-variable*—When you use an expression in a statement that is
embedded in an application program, you can refer to a variable
found in the program. A colon must precede the variable name to
distinguish the name from an SQL table or view *column-name*.

■ +¦-¦*¦/—You can combine multiple numeric expressions with
arithmetic operators that specify a calculation. If you use arithmetic operators, all expressions within an expression must be able
to be evaluated as numeric data types. In some implementations,
you can join alphanumeric constants using the special operator ¦¦,
which indicates concatenation.

## Examples:

To specify the average of a column named COST, enter the following function:

`AVG(COST)`

To specify one-half of the value of a column named PRICE, enter one of the following expressions:

`(COST * .5)`

or

`(COST / 2)`

To specify a character string that contains the name of the Acme Mail Order Company, enter the following literal:

`'Acme Mail Order Company'`

To specify a character string that contains a possessive noun (requiring an embedded apostrophe), enter the following literal:

`'Andy''s Hardware Store'`

## See Also:

Predicates, SELECT Statement, subSELECT Clause, and UPDATE Statement.

---

# FETCH Statement

## Syntax:

FETCH *cursor-name* INTO {*:host-variable*},...

## Description:

Fetches the values in the next row of the declared cursor into the specified list of host variables. The cursor must be open when you execute the FETCH statement.

## Notes:

- Only use this statement embedded in an application program. You must precede this statement with the EXEC SQL statement prefix and follow it with the SQL statement terminator appropriate to the application language (END-EXEC statement in COBOL).

- Unless you declared the cursor with an ORDER BY clause, the sequence of the returned rows is undefined in most implementations.

- The data type of the host variables must be compatible with the data type of the values returned by the cursor.

- If you specify fewer or more variables than are defined by the cursor, a warning indicator is returned to the program, and the SQLCODE is usually nonzero.

- When you reach the end of the logical table defined by the cursor, the host variables are unchanged, and the SQLCODE is usually 100.

- If an error occurs that yields invalid results or that makes the position of the cursor unpredictable, the cursor is closed.

## Examples:

In a COBOL program, to retrieve information about all customers who first did business in 1988, enter the following:

```
    EXEC SQL
    DECLARE NEWCUST CURSOR FOR
      SELECT CUSTNAME, ADDRESS
       FROM CUSTOMER
       WHERE FIRSDATE = '1988'
       ORDER BY ZIP ASC END-EXEC.
       ⋮
    EXEC SQL
    OPEN NEWCUST END-EXEC.
    ⋮
FETCH-LOOP.
    IF SQLCODE = 0
        EXEC SQL
        FETCH NEWCUST INTO :NEW-NAME, :NEW-ADDR END-EXEC.
        PERFORM PROCESS-CUST.
        GO TO FETCH-LOOP.
        ⋮
        EXEC SQL
        CLOSE NEWCUST END-EXEC.
```

In a C program, to retrieve information about all payments owed to the Acme Mail Order Company, enter the following:

```
EXEC SQL
DECLARE ACME_OWE CURSOR FOR
  SELECT PAYEENAME, ADDRESS, AMTOWED
  FROM ACCTSPAY
  WHERE PAYEENAME = 'Acme Mail Order Company';
  ⋮
```

*(continued)*

```
EXEC SQL
OPEN ACME_OWE;
⋮
while (SQLCODE = 0)
  {
  EXEC SQL
  FETCH ACME_OWE INTO :name, :address, :amount;
  process_owe();
  }
```

### See Also:

CLOSE Statement, DECLARE CURSOR Statement, and OPEN
Statement.

# FETCH Statement (Dynamic SQL)

## Syntax:

FETCH *cursor-name* USING DESCRIPTOR :*host-variable*

## Description:

Fetches the values in the next row of the declared cursor and sets the
pointers in the SQLDA that is specified by the *host-variable* name. The
cursor must be open when you execute the FETCH statement. Use this
form of the FETCH statement when you have dynamically retrieved
the variable descriptions from the SQL system by using a DESCRIBE
statement.

## Notes:

- Only use this statement embedded in an application program. You
  must precede this statement with the EXEC SQL statement prefix
  and follow it with the SQL statement terminator appropriate to the
  application language. (See END-EXEC Statement Terminator.)

- Unless you declared the cursor with an ORDER BY clause, the sequence of the returned rows is undefined in most implementations.

- The data type of the variables described in the SQLDA must be
  compatible with the data type of the values returned by the cursor.

- The *host-variable* must point to an SQLDA data area that is in a format accepted by your SQL system. The SQLDA must be initialized

by your application program prior to executing the FETCH statement. Usually, you initialize an SQLDA by executing a DESCRIBE statement.

■ If fewer or more variables are defined in the SQLDA than are defined by the cursor, a warning indicator is returned to the program, and the SQLCODE is usually nonzero.

■ When you reach the end of the logical table defined by the cursor, the variables defined by the SQLDA are unchanged, and the SQLCODE is usually 100.

■ If an error occurs that yields invalid results or that makes the position of the cursor unpredictable, the cursor is closed.

## Examples:

In a COBOL program, to dynamically retrieve information about all customers who first did business in 1988, enter the following:

```
WORKING-STORAGE SECTION.
    :
EXEC SQL
INCLUDE SQLDA END-EXEC.
    :
EXEC SQL
BEGIN DECLARE SECTION END-EXEC.
01   DYNAMIC-STATEMENT    PIC X(250) VALUE
-    'SELECT CUSTNAME, ADDRESS
-        '    FROM CUSTOMER
-        '    WHERE FIRSTDATE = ?
-        '    ORDER BY ZIP ASC'.
01   SELECT-DATE          PIC 9999.
EXEC SQL
END DECLARE SECTION END-EXEC.
    :
PROCEDURE DIVISION.
        :
        EXEC SQL
        PREPARE CUST-SEARCH FROM :DYNAMIC-STATEMENT END-EXEC.
        :
        EXEC SQL
        DESCRIBE CUST-SEARCH INTO :SQLDA END-EXEC.
        :
        EXEC SQL
        DECLARE NEWCUST CURSOR FOR CUST-SEARCH END-EXEC.
        :
        MOVE '1988' TO SELECT-DATE.
        EXEC SQL
        OPEN NEWCUST USING :SELECT-DATE END-EXEC.
        :
```

*(continued)*

```
FETCH-LOOP.
    IF SQLCODE = 0
        EXEC SQL
        FETCH NEWCUST USING DESCRIPTOR :SQLDA END-EXEC.
        PERFORM PROCESS-CUST.
        GO TO FETCH-LOOP.
    EXEC SQL
    CLOSE NEWCUST END-EXEC.
```

**Note:** The statement INCLUDE SQLDA (used in this example) is not supported for COBOL in every implementation. The example assumes that the INCLUDE directive creates a data structure named SQLDA. Some implementations of the INCLUDE directive allow you to provide a name for the SQLDA structure generated by the INCLUDE directive. See your product documentation for details.

In a C program, to use a cursor named NEWCUST to dynamically retrieve information about all customers who first did business in 1988 (also shown in the COBOL example), enter the following:

```
EXEC SQL
INCLUDE SQLDA;
:
EXEC SQL
BEGIN DECLARE SECTION;
char *dynamic_statement =
  "SELECT CUSTNAME, ADDRESS \
    FROM CUSTOMER \
    WHERE FIRSTDATE = ? \
    ORDER BY ZIP ASC";
char *select_date;
EXEC SQL
END DECLARE SECTION;
:
EXEC SQL
PREPARE CUST_SEARCH FROM :dynamic_statement;
:
EXEC SQL
DESCRIBE CUST_SEARCH INTO :SQLDA;
:
EXEC SQL
DECLARE NEWCUST CURSOR FOR CUST_SEARCH;
:
select_date = "1988";
EXEC SQL
OPEN NEWCUST USING :select_date;
:
```

```
while (SQLCODE <> 0)
  {
  EXEC SQL
  FETCH NEWCUST USING DESCRIPTOR :SQLDA;
  process_cust();
  }
EXEC SQL
CLOSE NEWCUST;
```

## See Also:

DECLARE CURSOR Statement (Dynamic SQL), DESCRIBE Statement
(Dynamic SQL), EXECUTE Statement (Dynamic SQL), INCLUDE
Directive, OPEN Statement (Dynamic SQL), and PREPARE Statement
(Dynamic SQL).

# Function: AVG

## Syntax:

AVG({[ALL] *expression* ¦ DISTINCT *column-name*})

## Description:

In a logical table defined by a SELECT statement or subSELECT
clause, creates a column value that is the numeric average of the
values in the *expression* or *column-name* specified. You can use the
GROUP BY clause to create an average for each group of rows selected
from the underlying tables or views.

## Notes:

■ You cannot use another function reference within the *expression*.
  Also, a *column-name* must not refer to a column in a view derived
  from a function.

■ If you use a column function (AVG, COUNT, MAX, MIN, or SUM)
  in the *select-list* of a SELECT statement, any other columns in the
  *select-list* must be derived using a column function, or the *column-
  name* must appear in a GROUP BY clause.

■ An *expression* must contain a reference to at least one *column-name*.

■ The *expression* or *column-name* must be a numeric data type.

■ Null values are not included in the calculation of the result.

■ If you specify DISTINCT *column-name*, duplicate values are eliminated before the average is calculated. For example, the function

AVG(DISTINCT *n*) — where the values of the column *n* in the selected rows are 2.0, 2.0, 4.5, and 5.5 — returns 4.0. (The duplicate 2.0 value is ignored.) AVG(ALL *n*) returns 3.5.

■ The data type of the result is generally the same as that of the *expression* or *column-name*. In most implementations, the result is a large integer if the *expression* or *column-name* is a small integer.

■ If the *expression* or *column-name* is an integer, the resulting average is usually truncated. For example, AVG(ALL *n*) — where *n* is an integer and the values of *n* in the selected rows are equal to 0, 1, and 1 — returns the value 0.

■ You can include a correlation name in an *expression* to indicate the table or view that contains the desired column; however, if you include a correlation name, you cannot include any operators in the *expression*.

## Examples:

To find the average amount owed to any vendor who sent a bill in October, enter the following:

```
SELECT AVG(AMTOWED)
  FROM ACCTSPAY
  WHERE MOBILL = 10
    AND AMTOWED > 0;
```

To find the average inventory cost of items currently on hand (not counting items that are not in stock), enter the following:

```
SELECT AVG(QTY * COST)
  FROM INVENTORY
  WHERE QTY > 0;
```

## See Also:

Expressions, GROUP BY Clause, HAVING Clause, SELECT Statement, subSELECT Clause, and Appendix (Common Data Types).

---

# Function: COUNT

## Syntax:

COUNT({* ¦ DISTINCT *column-name*})

## Description:

In a logical table defined by a SELECT statement or subSELECT clause, creates a column value that is equal to the number of rows in the result table or the number of distinct values in the specified *column-name*. You can use the GROUP BY clause to create a count for each group of rows selected from the underlying tables or views.

## Notes:

- If you use a column function (AVG, COUNT, MAX, MIN, or SUM) in the *select-list* of a SELECT statement, any other columns in the *select-list* must be derived using a column function, or the *column-name* must appear in a GROUP BY clause.

- If you specify DISTINCT *column-name*, duplicate values and nulls are eliminated before the count is obtained. For example, the function COUNT(DISTINCT *n*) — where the values of the column *n* in the selected rows are 2.0, 2.0, 4.5, and 5.5 — returns 3. (The duplicate 2.0 value is ignored.) COUNT(∗) returns 4.

- The data type of the result is a large integer.

## Examples:

To find the number of customers who first did business after the year 1985 and then group the listings by zip code, enter the following:

```
SELECT COUNT (*)
    FROM CUSTOMER
    WHERE FIRSTDATE > '1985'
    GROUP BY ZIP;
```

To find the number of different prices for items in the current inventory, enter the following:

```
SELECT COUNT(DISTINCT COST)
    FROM INVENTORY
    WHERE QTY > 0;
```

## See Also:

GROUP BY Clause, HAVING Clause, SELECT Statement, subSELECT Clause, and Appendix (Common Data Types).

# Function: MAX

## Syntax:

MAX({[ALL] *expression* ¦ DISTINCT *column-name*})

## Description:

In a logical table defined by a SELECT statement or subSELECT clause, creates a column value that is the maximum value in the *expression* or *column-name* specified. You can use the GROUP BY clause to create a maximum value for each group of rows selected from the underlying tables or views.

## Notes:

■ You cannot use another function reference within the *expression*. Also, a *column-name* must not refer to a column in a view derived from a function.

■ If you use a column function (AVG, COUNT, MAX, MIN, or SUM) in the *select-list* of a SELECT statement, any other columns in the *select-list* must be derived using a column function, or the *column-name* must appear in a GROUP BY clause.

■ An *expression* must contain a reference to at least one *column-name*.

■ Null values are not included in the determination of the result.

■ If you specify DISTINCT *column-name*, duplicate values are eliminated before the maximum value is determined.

■ The data type of the result is the same as that of the *expression* or *column-name*.

■ You can include a correlation name in an *expression* to indicate the table or view that contains the desired column; however, if you include a correlation name, you cannot include any operators in the *expression*.

## Examples:

To find the maximum amount owed to any vendor who sent a bill in October, enter the following:

```
SELECT MAX(AMTOWED)
  FROM ACCTSPAY
  WHERE MOBILL = 10;
```

To find the item currently on hand with the maximum inventory cost, enter the following:

```
SELECT MAX(QTY * COST)
  FROM INVENTORY;
```

## See Also:

Expressions, GROUP BY Clause, HAVING Clause, SELECT Statement, subSELECT Clause, and Appendix (Common Data Types).

# Function: MIN

## Syntax:

MIN({[ALL] *expression* ¦ DISTINCT *column-name*})

## Description:

In a logical table defined by a SELECT statement or subSELECT clause, creates a column value that is the minimum value in the *expression* or *column-name* specified. You can use the GROUP BY clause to create a minimum value for each group of rows selected from the underlying tables or views.

## Notes:

■ You cannot use another function reference within the *expression*. Also, a *column-name* must not refer to a column in a view derived from a function.

■ If you use a column function (AVG, COUNT, MAX, MIN, or SUM) in the *select-list* of a SELECT statement, any other columns in the *select-list* must be derived using a column function, or the *column-name* must appear in a GROUP BY clause.

■ An *expression* must contain a reference to at least one *column-name*.

■ Null values are not included in the determination of the result.

■ If you specify DISTINCT *column-name*, duplicate values are eliminated before the minimum value is determined.

■ The data type of the result is the same as that of the *expression* or *column-name*.

■ You can use a correlation name in an *expression* to indicate the table or view that contains the desired column; however, if you use a correlation name, you cannot include any operators in the *expression*.

## Examples:

To find the minimum amount owed to any vendor who sent a bill in October, enter the following:

```
SELECT MIN(AMTOWED)
  FROM ACCTSPAY
  WHERE MOBILL = 10
    AND AMTOWED > 0;
```

To find the item currently on hand with the minimum inventory cost (not counting items that are not in stock), enter the following:

```
SELECT MIN(QTY * COST)
  FROM INVENTORY
  WHERE QTY > 0;
```

### See Also:

Expressions, GROUP BY Clause, HAVING Clause, SELECT Statement, subSELECT Clause, and Appendix (Common Data Types).

---

# Function: SUM

## Syntax:

SUM({[ALL] *expression* ¦ DISTINCT *column-name*})

## Description:

In a logical table defined by a SELECT statement or subSELECT clause, creates a column value that is the numeric sum of the values in the *expression* or *column-name* specified. You can use the GROUP BY clause to create a sum for each group of rows selected from the under-lying tables or views.

## Notes:

- You cannot use another function reference within the *expression*. Also, a *column-name* must not refer to a column in a view derived from a function.

- If you use a column function (AVG, COUNT, MAX, MIN, or SUM) in the *select-list* of a SELECT statement, any other columns in the *select-list* must be derived using a column function, or the *column-name* must appear in a GROUP BY clause.

- An *expression* must contain a reference to at least one *column-name*.

- The *expression* or *column-name* must be a numeric data type.

- Null values are not included in the calculation of the result.

- If you specify DISTINCT *column-name*, duplicate values are elimi-nated before the sum is calculated. For example, the function SUM(DISTINCT *n*) — where the values of the column *n* in the selected rows are 2.0, 2.0, 4.5, and 5.5 — returns 12.0. (The duplicate 2.0 value is ignored.) SUM(ALL *n*) returns 14.0.

- The data type of the result is generally the same as that of the *expression* or *column-name*. In most implementations, the result is a large integer if the *expression* or *column-name* is a small integer.

- You can use a correlation name in an *expression* to indicate the table or view that contains the desired column; however, if you use a correlation name, you must not include any operators in the *expression*.

## Examples:

To find the total amount owed to all vendors who sent a bill in October, enter the following:

```
SELECT SUM(AMTOWED)
  FROM ACCTSPAY
  WHERE MOBILL = 10;
```

To find the total inventory cost of items currently on hand, enter the following:

```
SELECT SUM(QTY * COST)
  FROM INVENTORY;
```

## See Also:

Expressions, GROUP BY Clause, HAVING Clause, SELECT Statement, subSELECT Clause, and Appendix (Common Data Types).

# FROM Clause

## Syntax:

DELETE statement:
FROM {*table-name* ¦ *view-name*} [*correlation-name*]

SELECT statement, subSELECT clause:
FROM {{*table-name* ¦ *view-name*} [*correlation-name*]},...

## Description:

In a DELETE statement, specifies the table or view from which rows are deleted. In a SELECT statement or subSELECT clause, specifies the table(s) or view(s) from which rows are selected.

## Notes:

■ If you specify a *view-name* in a DELETE statement, the view must reference a single base table, must not contain an ORDER BY clause, and must not be constructed using the UNION, INTERSECT, or MINUS query operators. The view also must not contain a column function, the DISTINCT keyword, the GROUP BY or HAVING clauses, or a subSELECT clause that references the same base table as the DELETE statement.

■ You can optionally supply a *correlation-name* for each table or view name. You can use this *correlation-name* as an alias for the full table name when qualifying column names in the *select-list* or the WHERE clause and subclauses. If you are joining a table or a view to itself, you must use correlation names to clarify which copy of the table or view you are referring to in the *select-list*, join criteria, or selection criteria.

■ If you specify more than one table or view in the FROM clause of a SELECT statement or subSELECT clause, the SQL system logically creates the Cartesian product of all of the tables or views. (See the Joins section for explanation and examples of the Cartesian product.) The system then returns the rows in which the selection and join criteria specified in the WHERE clause are true.

■ Refer to your product documentation for rules on the formation of legal table or view names.

## Examples:

To delete rows from the customer table in which the last purchase date is before July 1988, enter the following:

```
DELETE FROM CUSTOMER A
  WHERE A.CUSTNO IN
    (SELECT CUSTNO FROM PURCHASE
      WHERE (LASTYEAR < 1988)
      OR (LASTYEAR = 1988
      AND LASTMONTH < 07);
```

To select information about customers and their purchases over $10, enter the following:

```
SELECT A.CUSTNO, A.CUSTNAME, A.ADDRESS,
 B.PURCHDATE, B.PURCHAMT, B.ITEMNO,
 C.ITEMNAME
  FROM CUSTOMER A, PURCHASE B, ITEMMAST C
  WHERE A.CUSTNO = B.CUSTNO
    AND B.ITEMNO = C.ITEMNO
    AND B.PURCHAMT > 10;
```

**See Also:**

DELETE Statement, Joins, SELECT Statement, and subSELECT Clause.

# GROUP BY Clause

## Syntax:

GROUP BY {*column-name* ¦ *column-number*},...

## Description:

In a SELECT statement, specifies columns used to form groups from the rows selected. Each group contains identical values in the specified column(s).

## Notes:

- A *column-name* in the GROUP BY clause can refer to any column from any table in the FROM clause, even if the column is not named in the *select-list*.

- Use a *column-number* to reference an unnamed column (such as an expression) in the *select-list*.

- If the GROUP BY clause is preceded by a WHERE clause, the system creates the groups from the rows selected after the application of the WHERE clause. In most implementations, the sequence in which you specify the WHERE and GROUP BY clauses is significant.

- In most implementations, you cannot use a GROUP BY clause in the subquery of a predicate.

- When you include a GROUP BY clause in a SELECT statement, the *select-list* must be made up of either column functions (AVG, COUNT, MAX, MIN, or SUM) or *column-names* specified in the GROUP BY clause.

- In most implementations, you cannot use a GROUP BY or HAVING clause in a SELECT statement or subSELECT clause if the SELECT statement or subSELECT clause contains a FROM clause that references a view that is defined using a GROUP BY or HAVING clause.

## Examples:

To find the largest order from any customer within each zip code, enter the following:

```
SELECT ZIP, MAX(PURCHAMT)
  FROM CUSTOMER A, PURCHASE B
  WHERE A.CUSTNO = B.CUSTNO
  GROUP BY ZIP;
```

To find the average and maximum amounts owed each month to suppliers in the state of Texas, enter the following:

```
SELECT MONTH, AVG(AMTOWED), MAX(AMTOWED)
  FROM SUPPLIER S, ACCTSPAY A
  WHERE S.SUPPNO = A.ACCTNO
    AND S.STATE = 'TX'
  GROUP BY MONTH;
```

## See Also:

Functions: AVG, COUNT, MAX, MIN, SUM; HAVING Clause, Search-condition, SELECT Statement, and WHERE Clause.

---

# HAVING Clause

## Syntax:

HAVING *search-condition*

## Description:

Specifies groups of rows that appear in the logical table defined by a SELECT statement. The *search-condition* applies to columns specified in a GROUP BY clause, to columns created by column functions, or to expressions containing column functions. If a group doesn't pass the *search-condition*, it is not included in the logical table.

## Notes:

■ If you do not include a GROUP BY clause, the *select-list* must be formed using column functions (AVG, COUNT, MAX, MIN, or SUM).

■ The difference between the HAVING clause and the WHERE clause is that WHERE *search-condition* applies to single rows whereas HAVING *search-condition* applies to groups of rows.

- If you include a GROUP BY clause preceding the HAVING clause, the *search-condition* applies to each of the groups formed by like values in the specified columns. If you do not include a GROUP BY clause, the *search-condition* applies to the entire logical table defined by the SELECT statement.

- In most implementations, you cannot use a GROUP BY or HAVING clause in a SELECT statement or subSELECT clause if the SELECT statement or subSELECT clause contains a FROM clause that references a view that is defined using a GROUP BY or HAVING clause.

- In some implementations, the system applies the HAVING clause to the results of the immediately preceding clauses. This means

  SELECT ... WHERE ... HAVING ... GROUP BY ...

  is processed differently than

  SELECT ... WHERE ... GROUP BY ... HAVING ...

  In other implementations, the system always applies the HAVING clause to the results of any GROUP BY, if present, regardless of the order of the clauses. Consult your product documentation for details.

## Examples:

To find the largest purchase from each group (categorized by zip code) whose largest purchase is less than the average of purchases by all customers, enter the following:

```
SELECT ZIP, MAX(PURCHAMT)
  FROM CUSTOMER A, PURCHASE B
  WHERE A.CUSTNO = B.CUSTNO
  GROUP BY ZIP
  HAVING MAX(PURCHAMT) <
    (SELECT AVG(PURCHAMT) FROM PURCHASE);
```

To find the average and maximum amounts owed to suppliers in the state of Texas every month in which the maximum amount owed is under $1,000, enter the following:

```
SELECT MOBILL, AVG(AMTOWED), MAX(AMTOWED)
  FROM SUPPLIER S, ACCTSPAY A
  WHERE S.SUPPNO = A.ACCTNO
    AND S.STATE = 'TX'
  GROUP BY MOBILL
  HAVING MAX(AMTOWED) < 1000;
```

## See Also:

Functions: AVG, COUNT, MAX, MIN, SUM; GROUP BY Clause, Search-condition, SELECT Statement, and WHERE Clause.

# INCLUDE Directive

## Syntax:

INCLUDE {SQLCA ¦ SQLDA ¦ *member-name*}

## Description:

Generates within an application's source code data structures that define the format of the SQL Communications Area (SQLCA) or SQL Descriptor Area (SQLDA), or copies the specified *member-name* data structure from a source library, which the SQL precompiler accesses.

## Notes:

- Only use this statement embedded in an application program. You must precede this statement with the EXEC SQL statement prefix and follow it with the SQL statement terminator appropriate to the application language. (See END-EXEC Statement Terminator.)

- In most implementations, you cannot include an SQLCA or SQLDA within an SQL declare section.

- Format of the SQLCA (and all other codes) is implementation specific, but the SQLCA generally contains the variable SQLCODE that you can use to test for satisfactory completion of SQL commands. By convention, the value 0 (zero) in SQLCODE indicates successful completion, and the value 100 indicates that no rows were found or that it is the end of a set. All other codes are implementation specific.

- In some implementations, the precompiler automatically generates an SQLCA in the working storage section of a COBOL program if you do not provide an INCLUDE SQLCA directive.

- Format of the SQLDA is implementation specific. Some implementations do not allow INCLUDE SQLDA in a COBOL program. Other implementations require that you provide in the following form a structure name and a count of the variables to be described:

  INCLUDE SQLDA (*sqlda-name*,[*item-count*])

  Consult your product documentation for details.

- Not all implementations allow the use of a *member-name* in the INCLUDE directive. Each implementation that allows INCLUDE *member-name* has specific requirements about defining the source library to the precompiler. Consult your product documentation for details.

## Examples:

In a COBOL program, to generate an SQLCA, enter the following:

```
WORKING-STORAGE SECTION.
⋮
EXEC SQL
INCLUDE SQLCA END-EXEC.
```

In a C program, to generate an SQLDA, enter the following:

```
EXEC SQL
INCLUDE SQLDA;
```

## See Also:

BEGIN DECLARE SECTION Directive, END DECLARE SECTION Directive, END-EXEC Statement Terminator, and EXEC SQL Statement Prefix.

# INSERT Statement

## Syntax:

INSERT INTO {*table-name* ¦ *view-name*} [({*column-name*},...)]
  {VALUES({*literal* ¦ :*host-variable* ¦ NULL},...) ¦
  *select-statement*}

## Description:

Inserts one or more new rows into the specified table or view. When you use the VALUES clause, only a single row is inserted. If you use a *select-statement*, the number of rows inserted equals the number of rows returned by the *select-statement*.

## Notes:

- You can embed this statement in an application program when you precede it with the required EXEC SQL statement prefix and follow it with the SQL statement terminator appropriate to the application language. (See END-EXEC Statement Terminator.)

- Some SQL implementations support only a *table-name* in the INTO clause. Generally, for a *view-name* to be supported in an INTO clause, the view must be constructed from only one base table and cannot be a read-only view.

- You cannot insert into a view that was created with an ORDER BY clause or a UNION operation.

- You cannot insert into a view created with a SELECT statement that includes a column function (AVG, COUNT, MAX, MIN, or SUM), an arithmetic expression, the DISTINCT keyword, the GROUP BY or HAVING clauses, or a subSELECT clause that references the same base table as the SELECT statement.

- You can insert into a view only if all columns are declared NOT NULL in the underlying table.

- If you do not include a *column-name* list, you must supply values for all columns defined in the table or view in the order in which they were declared in the CREATE TABLE or CREATE VIEW statements. If you embed this statement in an application program, the system assumes the *column-name* list that existed in the table or view at the time the application program was compiled.

- If you include a *column-name* list, you must supply values for all columns in the list, and the values must be compatible with the receiving column attributes.

- If you supply a *column-name* list, you must include in the list all columns declared NOT NULL in the underlying table. Some implementations that provide for the definition of default values allow you to omit those NOT NULL columns that have a default value declared.

- If you supply values by using a *select-statement*, the statement's FROM clause cannot have the target table of the insert as its *table-name* or as an underlying table. The target table also cannot be used in any subSELECT clause.

- Many systems provide the ability to define column value constraints, edit routines, or referential integrity checks. Any values that you insert must pass these validations before the system accepts the new row.

- If you are inserting into a view that was declared using the WITH CHECK OPTION clause, the inserted row must pass the view selection criteria.

- If you are inserting into a view that does not include the WITH CHECK OPTION clause, the row must pass only the validation criteria of the underlying table. Note that you cannot retrieve the inserted row using the view if the row does not pass the view selection criteria.

## Examples:

To insert a new row in the table CUSTOMER, enter the following:

```
INSERT INTO CUSTOMER (CUSTNO, CUSTNAME, ADDRESS, CITY,
  STATE, ZIP, FIRSDATE)
  VALUES (399,'Chris Date','P.O. Box 1',
    'San Jose','CA',95000,881205);
```

To retrieve from the table CUSTOMER and insert into a temporary table a list of customers who live in the state of Oregon, enter the following:

```
INSERT INTO TEMPCUST
  SELECT CUSTNAME, ADDRESS
  FROM CUSTOMER
  WHERE STATE = 'OR';
```

### See Also:

DELETE Statement, SELECT Statement, subSELECT Clause, CREATE TABLE Statement (Data Definition Language), and CREATE VIEW Statement (Data Definition Language).

# INTERSECT Query Operator

### Syntax:

*select-statement*
  INTERSECT
*select-statement*
[ORDER BY {integer[ASC ¦ DESC]},...]

### Description:

Produces a logical table containing the rows returned by the first *select-statement* that are identical to the rows returned by the second *select-statement*.

### Notes:

- The INTERSECT query operator is an extension to ANSI standard SQL and is not found in all implementations.

- You must not use an ORDER BY clause in SELECT statements that are joined by query operators; however, you can include at the end of a statement a single ORDER BY clause that uses one or more query operators. This action will apply the specified order to the result of the entire statement.

- You cannot use the FOR UPDATE clause in a statement that includes a query operator.

- The tables returned by each SELECT statement must contain an equal number of columns, and each column must have identical attributes.

- Column names in the result table are undefined. You can refer to result columns (for example, in an ORDER BY clause) by position number.

- Most implementations that support query operators (INTERSECT, MINUS, or UNION) allow you to combine multiple SELECT statements using these operators to obtain complex results. You can use parentheses to influence the sequence in which the system applies the operators. For example,

  SELECT ... UNION (SELECT ... INTERSECT SELECT ...)

## Example:

To find all suppliers in the state of Massachusetts who are also customers and sort the resulting table by zip code, enter the following:

```
SELECT CUSTNAME, ZIP
  FROM CUSTOMER WHERE STATE = 'MA'
INTERSECT
SELECT SUPNAME, ZIP
  FROM SUPPLIER WHERE STATE = 'MA'
ORDER BY 2;
```

## See Also:

MINUS Query Operator, ORDER BY Clause, SELECT Statement, and UNION Query Operator.

# Joins

## Description:

Much of the power of SQL derives from its ability to combine information (join) from several tables. In the current implementations of SQL, you initiate a join by specifying more than one table or view in the FROM clause of a SELECT statement. The system then begins the selection process by logically creating the Cartesian product of all the rows in the tables or views. (For efficiency's sake, all systems optimize the selection process by first applying selection criteria found in the WHERE or HAVING clauses in order to eliminate many rows from the Cartesian product before it is formed.) The Cartesian product of multiple tables or views contains all the rows in table or view "A" paired with all the rows in table or view "B" paired with view "C", and so on.

The number of rows in the Cartesian product is simply the product of the number of rows found in each table or view (#A × #B × #C × ...).

For example, assume two existing tables appear as the following:

**SUPPLIER**

| SUPPNO | SUPPNAME |
|--------|----------|
| 0001 | Acme Mail Order Co. |
| 0002 | Codd & Date Consulting |
| 0003 | Suzanne's Bookstore |
| 0004 | Computer Peripherals |

**ACCTSPAY**

| ACCTNO | PAYEENAME | AMTOWED |
|--------|-----------|---------|
| 0001 | Acme Mail Order Co. | 6.78 |
| 0002 | Chris Date | 375.00 |
| 0003 | Suzanne's Bookstore | 8.16 |
| 0003 | Suzanne's Bookstore | 23.95 |

The Cartesian product would be the following:

| SUPPNO | SUPPNAME | ACCTNO | PAYEENAME | AMTOWED |
|--------|----------|--------|-----------|---------|
| 0001 | Acme Mail Order Co. | 0001 | Acme Mail Order Co. | 6.78 |
| 0001 | Acme Mail Order Co. | 0002 | Chris Date | 375.00 |
| 0001 | Acme Mail Order Co. | 0003 | Suzanne's Bookstore | 8.16 |
| 0001 | Acme Mail Order Co. | 0003 | Suzanne's Bookstore | 23.95 |
| 0002 | Codd & Date Consulting | 0001 | Acme Mail Order Co. | 6.78 |
| 0002 | Codd & Date Consulting | 0002 | Chris Date | 375.00 |
| 0002 | Codd & Date Consulting | 0003 | Suzanne's Bookstore | 8.16 |
| 0002 | Codd & Date Consulting | 0003 | Suzanne's Bookstore | 23.95 |
| 0003 | Suzanne's Bookstore | 0001 | Acme Mail Order Co. | 6.78 |
| 0003 | Suzanne's Bookstore | 0002 | Chris Date | 375.00 |

*(continued)*

| SUPPNO | SUPPNAME | ACCTNO | PAYEENAME | AMTOWED |
|--------|----------|--------|-----------|---------|
| 0003 | Suzanne's Bookstore | 0003 | Suzanne's Bookstore | 8.16 |
| 0003 | Suzanne's Bookstore | 0003 | Suzanne's Bookstore | 23.95 |
| 0004 | Computer Peripherals | 0001 | Acme Mail Order Co. | 6.78 |
| 0004 | Computer Peripherals | 0002 | Chris Date | 375.00 |
| 0004 | Computer Peripherals | 0003 | Suzanne's Bookstore | 8.16 |
| 0004 | Computer Peripherals | 0003 | Suzanne's Bookstore | 23.95 |

Note that executing a SELECT statement with multiple tables in the FROM clause and with no other selection criteria (WHERE, GROUP BY, HAVING) results in the Cartesian product shown.

To obtain a meaningful result, you need to include join criteria in the WHERE clause, thus eliminating in the Cartesian product rows that contain superfluous information. In this example, you would probably include a WHERE SUPPLIER.SUPPNO = ACCTSPAY.ACCTNO clause that produces the following result:

| SUPPNO | SUPPNAME | ACCTNO | PAYEENAME | AMTOWED |
|--------|----------|--------|-----------|---------|
| 0001 | Acme Mail Order Co. | 0001 | Acme Mail Order Co. | 6.78 |
| 0002 | Codd & Date Consulting | 0002 | Chris Date | 375.00 |
| 0003 | Suzanne's Bookstore | 0003 | Suzanne's Bookstore | 8.16 |
| 0003 | Suzanne's Bookstore | 0003 | Suzanne's Bookstore | 23.95 |

Providing the WHERE clause in this form creates an Equijoin (*Equi-* meaning equal). You can also specify other comparison operators such as greater than (>) or less than (<) to produce non-Equijoins, but doing so in this example would not prove useful.

This Equijoin example is also called an Inner Join because it includes only rows that have matching column values from both tables. If you enter a SELECT * (all columns) on the above join, the system returns the matched value twice—once in the SUPPNO column and once in the ACCTNO column. If, however, you enter the following:

```
SELECT SUPPNO, SUPPNAME, PAYEENAME, AMTOWED
  FROM SUPPLIER, ACCTSPAY
  WHERE SUPPNO = ACCTNO
```

you receive a result table that does not contain the duplicate matched value. This is a Natural Inner Join.

Sometimes it is useful to know which rows from one table are not matched in a related table. For example, you might want to know which suppliers are not reflected in the accounts-payable table (you don't owe them any money) in addition to those who are. Unfortunately, standard SQL does not offer a simple way to create the table that provides this information. Another type of join—an Outer Join—is needed. Some implementations provide for an Outer Join through a special indicator character on the join predicate in the WHERE clause:

```
SELECT SUPPNO, SUPPNAME, PAYEENAME, AMTOWED
  FROM SUPPLIER, ACCTSPAY
  WHERE SUPPNO = ACCTNO (+)
```

The ANSI committee has also proposed an extension to the standard as follows:

```
SELECT COALESCE(SUPPNO,ACCTNO) AS NUMBER, SUPPNAME,
  PAYEENAME, AMTOWED
  FROM SUPPLIER LEFT JOIN ACCTSPAY ON SUPPNO = ACCTNO
```

Both examples of the Outer Join should return the following:

| NUMBER | SUPPNAME | PAYEENAME | AMTOWED |
|--------|----------|-----------|---------|
| 0001 | Acme Mail Order Co. | Acme Mail Order Co. | 6.78 |
| 0002 | Codd & Date Consulting | Chris Date | 375.00 |
| 0003 | Suzanne's Bookstore | Suzanne's Bookstore | 8.16 |
| 0003 | Suzanne's Bookstore | Suzanne's Bookstore | 23.95 |
| 0004 | Computer Peripherals | (NULL) | (NULL) |

## See Also:

FROM Clause, HAVING Clause, SELECT Statement, and WHERE Clause.

# MINUS Query Operator

## Syntax:

*select-statement*
MINUS
*select-statement*
[ORDER BY {*integer* [ASC ¦ DESC]},...]

## Description:

Produces a result table containing the rows returned by the first *select-statement* that are not found in the rows returned by the second *select-statement*.

## Notes:

- The MINUS query operator is an extension to ANSI standard SQL and is not found in all implementations.

- You must not use the ORDER BY clause in SELECT statements that are joined by query operators; however, you can include at the end of the statement a single ORDER BY clause that uses one or more query operators. This action will apply the specified order to the result of the entire statement.

- You cannot use the FOR UPDATE clause in a statement that includes a query operator.

- The tables returned by each SELECT statement must have an equal number of columns, and each column must contain identical attributes.

- Column names in the result table are undefined. You can refer to result columns (for example, in an ORDER BY clause) by position number.

- Most implementations that support query operators (INTERSECT, MINUS, or UNION) allow you to combine multiple SELECT statements using these operators to obtain complex results. You can use parentheses to influence the sequence in which the system applies the operators. For example,

   SELECT ... UNION (SELECT ... MINUS SELECT ...)

## Example:

To find all customers in the state of Massachusetts except those who are also suppliers, and to sort the list by zip code, enter the following:

```
SELECT CUSTNAME, ZIP
  FROM CUSTOMER WHERE STATE = 'MA'
MINUS
SELECT SUPNAME, ZIP
  FROM SUPPLIER WHERE STATE = 'MA'
ORDER BY 2;
```

## See Also:

INTERSECT Query Operator, ORDER BY Clause, SELECT Statement, and UNION Query Operator.

# OPEN Statement

## Syntax:

OPEN *cursor-name*

## Description:

Opens a cursor declared in an application program. A cursor is a logical pointer to rows within a logical table that is defined by a SELECT statement within a DECLARE CURSOR statement. Executing an OPEN creates the logical table and places the cursor before the first row in the table.

## Notes:

- Only use this statement embedded in an application program. You must precede this statement with the EXEC SQL statement prefix and follow it with the SQL statement terminator appropriate to the application language. (See END-EXEC Statement Terminator.)

- The cursor must be closed when your program executes this statement; otherwise an error is returned to your program. You can close an open cursor in a program by using a CLOSE statement or a COMMIT WORK statement. Note that all cursors are closed when a program is initiated.

- To update the logical table associated with an open cursor, you must include in the DECLARE CURSOR statement a FOR UPDATE clause that specifies the columns eligible to be updated.

- To specify an order for the rows presented to your application program through an open cursor, you must include in the DECLARE CURSOR statement an ORDER BY clause that specifies the columns that contain values on which the cursor is to be ordered. If you do not specify an ORDER BY clause, the sequence in which the system returns the rows is undefined.

■ You cannot update the logical table associated with a cursor declared with an ORDER BY clause or with any query operator.

■ You cannot update the logical table associated with a cursor declared with a SELECT statement that includes a column function, the DISTINCT keyword, the GROUP BY or the HAVING clauses, or a subSELECT clause that references the same base table as the SELECT statement.

■ You cannot update the logical table associated with a cursor declared with a SELECT statement that references more than one table or that references a read-only view in the FROM clause.

## Examples:

In a COBOL program, to declare and open a logical table that lists in ascending order by zip code only those customers who first did business in 1988, enter the following:

```
EXEC SQL
DECLARE NEWCUST CURSOR FOR
  SELECT CUSTNAME, ADDRESS
   FROM CUSTOMER
   WHERE FIRSDATE = '1988'
   ORDER BY ZIP ASC END-EXEC.
  ⋮
EXEC SQL
OPEN NEWCUST END-EXEC.
```

In a C program, to declare and open a logical table that includes all payments owed to the Acme Mail Order Company and that allows the check number to be inserted, enter the following:

```
EXEC SQL
DECLARE ACMEOWE CURSOR FOR
  SELECT PAYEENAME, ADDRESS, AMTOWED, CHECKNUM
   FROM ACCTSPAY
   WHERE PAYEENAME = 'Acme Mail Order Company'
   FOR UPDATE OF CHECKNUM;
  ⋮
EXEC SQL
OPEN ACMEOWE;
```

## See Also:

CLOSE Statement, DECLARE CURSOR Statement, DELETE...WHERE CURRENT OF Statement, END-EXEC Statement Terminator, EXEC SQL Statement Prefix, FETCH Statement, INTERSECT Query Operator, MINUS Query Operator, SELECT Statement, subSELECT Clause,

UNION Query Operator, and UPDATE...WHERE CURRENT OF Statement.

# OPEN Statement (Dynamic SQL)

## Syntax:

OPEN *cursor-name*
  [USING {*:host-variable*},... !
  USING DESCRIPTOR *:host-variable*]

## Description:

Opens a cursor dynamically declared and prepared in an application program. A cursor is a logical pointer to rows within a logical table defined by the prepared SELECT statement and referred to in a DECLARE CURSOR statement. Executing an OPEN creates the logical table and places the cursor immediately before the first row in the table. If you include parameter indicators—a question mark (?) in most implementations—in the SELECT statement, you must provide substitution values through either a list of host variables or a host variable that contains an SQLDA structure that describes the substitution variables.

## Notes:

■ Only use this statement embedded in an application program. You must precede this statement with the EXEC SQL statement prefix and follow it with the SQL statement terminator appropriate to the application language. (See END-EXEC Statement Terminator.)

■ The cursor must be closed when your program executes this statement; otherwise an error is returned to your program. You can close an open cursor in a program by using a CLOSE statement or a COMMIT WORK statement. Note that all cursors are closed when a program is initiated.

■ To update the logical table associated with an open cursor, you must include in the DECLARE CURSOR statement a FOR UPDATE clause that specifies the columns eligible to be updated.

■ To specify an order for the rows presented to your application program through an open cursor, you must include in the DECLARE CURSOR statement an ORDER BY clause that specifies the columns that contain values on which the cursor is to be ordered. If you do not specify an ORDER BY clause, the sequence in which the system returns the rows is undefined.

- You cannot update the logical table associated with a cursor declared using an ORDER BY clause or any query operator.

- You cannot update the logical table associated with a cursor declared using a SELECT statement that includes a column function, the DISTINCT keyword, the GROUP BY or the HAVING clauses, or a subSELECT clause that references the same base table as the SELECT statement.

- You cannot update the logical table associated with a cursor declared using a SELECT statement that references more than one table or a read-only view in the FROM clause.

## Examples:

In a COBOL program, to dynamically declare and open a logical table that lists in ascending order by zip code only those customers who first did business in the year 1988 (the date provided as a parameter to an OPEN statement), enter the following:

```
WORKING-STORAGE SECTION.
  ⋮
EXEC SQL
BEGIN DECLARE SECTION END-EXEC.
  01   DYNAMIC-STATEMENT    PIC X(250) VALUE
  -      'SELECT CUSTNAME, ADDRESS
  -         'FROM CUSTOMER
  -         'WHERE FIRSTDATE = ?
  -         'ORDER BY ZIP ASC'.
  01   SELECT-DATE          PIC 9999.
EXEC SQL
END DECLARE SECTION END-EXEC.
  ⋮
PROCEDURE DIVISION.
     ⋮
    EXEC SQL
    PREPARE CUST-SEARCH FROM :DYNAMIC-STATEMENT END-EXEC.
     ⋮
    EXEC SQL
    DECLARE NEWCUST CURSOR FOR CUST-SEARCH END-EXEC.
     ⋮
    MOVE '1988' TO SELECT-DATE.
    EXEC SQL
    OPEN NEWCUST USING :SELECT-DATE END-EXEC.
```

In a C program, to dynamically declare and open a logical table that includes all bills owed to the Acme Mail Order Company and that allows the check number to be inserted, enter the following:

```
EXEC SQL
BEGIN DECLARE SECTION;
    char *dynam_select =
        "SELECT PAYEENAME, ADDRESS, AMTOWED, CHECKNUM \
            FROM ACCTSPAY \
            WHERE PAYEENAME = 'Acme Mail Order Company' \
            FOR UPDATE OF CHECKNUM";
EXEC SQL
END DECLARE SECTION;
    ⋮
EXEC SQL
PREPARE UPDTACCT FROM :dynam_select;
    ⋮
EXEC SQL
DECLARE ACMEOWE CURSOR FOR UPDTACCT;
    ⋮
EXEC SQL
OPEN ACMEOWE;
```

### See Also:

CLOSE Statement, DECLARE CURSOR Statement (Dynamic SQL), DELETE...WHERE CURRENT OF Statement, END-EXEC Statement Terminator, EXEC SQL Statement Prefix, FETCH Statement (Dynamic SQL), PREPARE Statement (Dynamic SQL), SELECT Statement, subSELECT Clause, and UPDATE...WHERE CURRENT OF Statement.

---

# ORDER BY Clause

### Syntax:

ORDER BY {{*column-name* ¦ *column-number*} [ASC ¦ DESC]},...

### Description:

Specifies the sequence of rows to be returned by an interactive SELECT statement or by a SELECT statement in a DECLARE CURSOR or INSERT statement.

### Notes:

■ You specify the column(s) on whose value the rows returned are ordered by using column names or relative column numbers (1 is the first column). Note that you can use a combination of names and numbers in the clause.

- A column name can be ambiguous because the same name might appear in a *select-list* more than once, or different column names might appear in the same position through an INTERSECT, MINUS, or UNION operation, which causes the column names in the result table to be undefined. If the *column-name* is ambiguous, you must use a relative column number in the ORDER BY clause.

- You can specify multiple columns in the ORDER BY clause. The list is ordered primarily by the first *column-name* or *column-number*. If rows exist for which the values of that column are equal, they are then ordered by the next *column-name* or *column-number* on the ORDER BY list.

- You can specify ascending (ASC) or descending (DESC) ordering for each column. If you do not choose ASC or DESC, ASC is assumed.

- Use of an ORDER BY clause in a SELECT statement is the only means of defining the sequence of the returned rows.

## Examples:

To select customers who first did business in 1988 and list them in ascending order by zip code, enter the following:

```
SELECT CUSTNAME, ADDRESS FROM CUSTOMER
  WHERE FIRSDATE = '1988'
  ORDER BY ZIP ASC;
```

To find all suppliers and all customers in the state of Massachusetts and list them in descending order by zip code, enter the following:

```
SELECT CUSTNAME, ZIP
  FROM CUSTOMER WHERE STATE = 'MA'
UNION
SELECT SUPPNAME, ZIP
  FROM SUPPLIER WHERE STATE = 'MA'
  ORDER BY 2 DESC;
```

## See Also:

DECLARE CURSOR Statement, INSERT Statement, INTERSECT Query Operator, MINUS Query Operator, SELECT Statement, and UNION Query Operator.

# Predicate: BETWEEN

## Syntax:

*expression* [NOT] BETWEEN *expression* AND *expression*

## Description:

Compares a value with a range of values.

## Notes:

■ The data types of all expressions must be compatible.

■ The result of the comparison of alphanumeric literals depends on the internal character set supported by the system (ASCII or EBCDIC). Consult your product documentation for details.

■ Let *a*, *b*, and *c* be expressions. Then, in terms of other predicates, *a* BETWEEN *b* AND *c* is equivalent to the following:

$a >= b$ AND $a <= c$

*a* NOT BETWEEN *b* AND *c* is equivalent to the following:

$a < b$ OR $a > c$

■ The result is unknown if any of the expressions is NULL.

## Example:

To determine if the average of QTY multiplied by COST is greater than or equal to $500 and less than or equal to $10,000, enter the following:

```
AVG(QTY * COST) BETWEEN 500 AND 10000
```

## See Also:

Expressions, SELECT Statement, subSELECT Clause, and WHERE Clause.

# Predicate: Comparison

## Syntax:

*expression* { = ¦ <> ¦ > ¦ < ¦ >= ¦ <= }
{*expression* ¦ *subselect-clause*}

## Description:

Compares the values of two expressions or the value of an *expression* and a single value returned by a subSELECT clause.

## Notes:

■ The data type of the first *expression* must be compatible with the data type of the second *expression* or with the value returned by the subSELECT clause.

- The result of the comparison of alphanumeric literals depends on the internal character set supported by the system (ASCII or EBCDIC). Consult your product documentation for details.
- If the subSELECT clause returns no rows or more than one row, an error is returned except when the *select-list* of the subSELECT clause is COUNT(∗) (in which case the return of multiple rows yields one value).
- If either the first *expression*, the second *expression*, or the sub-SELECT clause evaluates to NULL, the result of the comparison is unknown.

### Examples:

To determine if FIRSDATE is equal to '1988', enter the following:

```
FIRSDATE = '1988'
```

To determine if CHECKNUM is not equal to 50, enter the following:

```
CHECKNUM <> 50
```

To determine if AMTOWED is greater than 0, enter the following:

```
AMTOWED > 0
```

To determine if LASTMONTH is less than 7, enter the following:

```
LASTMONTH < 7
```

To determine if the maximum value for PURCHAMT in the group is less than the average PURCHAMT found in the PURCHASE table, enter the following:

```
MAX(PURCHAMT) < (SELECT AVG(PURCHAMT) FROM PURCHASE)
```

### See Also:

Expressions, SELECT Statement, subSELECT Clause, and WHERE Clause.

# Predicate: EXISTS

### Syntax:

EXISTS *subselect-clause*

### Description:

Tests the existence of at least one row that satisfies the selection criteria in a subSELECT clause.

## Notes:

- The result cannot be unknown. If the subSELECT clause returns at least one row, the result is true; otherwise, the result is false.

- The subSELECT clause need not return values for this predicate; therefore, you can list any columns in the *select-list* that exist in the underlying tables or views (including *).

## Example:

To find the inventory item name and supplier name for any item that has an inventory cost of less than $50, enter the following:

```
SELECT ITEMNAME, SUPPNAME
  FROM INVENTORY I, SUPPLIER S
  WHERE EXISTS
    (SELECT * FROM INVENTORY I2
      WHERE I.ITEMNO = I2.ITEMNO
      AND (I2.QTY * I2.COST) < 50);
```

**Note:** In the above example, the inner subSELECT clause makes an outer reference to the INVENTORY table in the SELECT statement by specifically referring to the *correlation-name* 'I' (I.ITEMNO in the WHERE clause of the subSELECT clause). This forces the subSELECT clause to be evaluated for every row in the SELECT statement, which might not be the most efficient way to achieve the desired result.

## See Also:

Expression, SELECT Statement, subSELECT Clause, and WHERE Clause.

# Predicate: IN

## Syntax:

*expression* [NOT] IN
{*subselect-clause* ╎ ({:*host-variable*╎*literal*},...) ╎ *expression*}

## Description:

Determines if a value is equal to any of the values or is unequal to all values in a set returned from a subSELECT clause or provided in a list of values.

## Notes:

■ The data types of all expressions, host variables, literals, or the column returned by the subSELECT clause must be compatible.

■ The result of the comparison of alphanumeric values depends on the internal character set supported by the system (ASCII or EBCDIC). Consult your product documentation for details.

■ If the expression is NULL or any value returned by the subSELECT clause is NULL, the result is unknown.

In terms of other predicates,

■ *expression* IN *expression* is equivalent to the following:

*expression = expression*

*expression* IN *subselect-clause* is equivalent to the following:

*expression* = ANY *subselect-clause*

*expression* IN (*a*, *b*, *c*, ...), where *a*, *b*, and *c* are literals, is equivalent to the following:

(*expression = a*) OR (*expression = b*) OR
(*expression = c*) ...

*expression* NOT IN ... is equivalent to the following:

NOT (*expression* IN ... )

## Examples:

To determine if STATE is on the West Coast, enter the following:

```
STATE IN ('CA', 'OR', 'WA')
```

To determine if CUSTNO is the same as any SUPPNO in Florida, enter the following:

```
CUSTNO IN (SELECT SUPPNO FROM SUPPLIER
           WHERE STATE = 'FL')
```

## See Also:

Expressions, SELECT Statement, subSELECT Clause, and WHERE Clause.

# Predicate: LIKE

## Syntax:

*column-name* [NOT] LIKE {:*host-variable* ¦ *string-literal*}
[ESCAPE {:*host-variable* ¦ *string-literal*}]

## Description:

Searches for strings that match a pattern.

## Notes:

■ Two special characters are available to construct the comparison string in the *host-variable* or *string-literal*. The percent sign (%) indicates that the string being compared to the *string-literal* can have any number of characters (or none) in the position the percent sign occupies and still match the *string-literal*. The underscore (_) indicates that the string being compared to the *string-literal* can have any one character in the position occupied by the underscore.

■ Use the character specified by the ESCAPE clause preceding a percent sign (%) or an underscore (_) in the comparison string to test for the existence of these special characters.

■ Both the data type of the specified column and the *host-variable* or *string-literal* must be character strings.

■ If the column specified by *column-name* contains a NULL, the result is undefined.

■ The result of the comparison of alphanumeric literals depends on the internal character set supported by the system (ASCII or EBCDIC). Consult your product documentation for details.

■ Comparison of two empty strings or an empty string with the special character '%' evaluates true.

## Examples:

To determine if CUSTNAME is at least four characters long and begins with 'Smi', enter the following:

```
CUSTNAME LIKE 'Smi_%'
```

To test whether SUPPNAME starts with the string 'Max %age Discount', enter the following:

```
SUPPNAME LIKE 'Max =%age Discount%' ESCAPE '='
```

## See Also:

Expressions, SELECT Statement, subSELECT Clause, and WHERE Clause.

# Predicate: NULL

## Syntax:

*expression* IS [NOT] NULL

## Description:

Determines if the expression evaluates to NULL. This predicate evaluates only to true or false and will not evaluate to unknown.

## Example:

To determine if the customer phone-number column has never been filled, enter the following:

```
PHONENO IS NULL
```

## See Also:

Expressions, SELECT Statement, subSELECT Clause, and WHERE Clause.

---

# Predicate: Quantified

## Syntax:

*expression* { = ¦ <> ¦ > ¦ < ¦ >= ¦ <= }
[SOME¦ANY¦ALL] *subselect-clause*}

## Description:

Compares the value of an *expression* to some, any, or all values of a single column returned by a subSELECT clause.

## Notes:

■ The data type of the first *expression* must be compatible with the data type of the value returned by the subSELECT clause.

■ The result of the comparison of alphanumeric literals depends on the internal character set supported by the system (ASCII or EBCDIC). Consult your product documentation for details.

■ When using ALL, the predicate is true if the comparison is true for all the values returned by the subSELECT clause. If the *expression* or any of the values returned by the subSELECT clause is NULL, the result is unknown.

- When using either SOME or ANY, the predicate is true if the comparison is true for any of the values returned by the subSELECT clause. If the *expression* is a NULL value, the result is unknown. If the subSELECT returns no values, the predicate is false.

## Examples:

To determine if AMTOWED is greater than all amounts owed to any supplier from the state of Illinois, enter the following:

```
AMTOWED > ALL (SELECT AMTOWED
               FROM SUPPLIER S, ACCTSPAY A
               WHERE S.SUPPNO = A.ACCTNO
               AND S.STATE = 'IL')
```

To determine if CUSTNAME is equal to any SUPPNAME in the state of Colorado, enter the following:

```
CUSTNAME = ANY (SELECT SUPPNAME FROM SUPPLIER
                WHERE STATE = 'CO')
```

## See Also:

Expressions, SELECT Statement, subSELECT Clause, and WHERE Clause.

# PREPARE Statement (Dynamic SQL)

## Syntax:

PREPARE *statement-name* FROM :*host-variable*

## Description:

Dynamically compiles and prepares for execution an SQL statement as defined by the character string stored in the *host-variable*.

## Notes:

- Only use this statement embedded in an application program. You must precede this statement with the EXEC SQL statement prefix and follow it with the SQL statement terminator appropriate to the application language. (See END-EXEC Statement Terminator.)

- You can dynamically prepare any SQL statement except the following: CLOSE, DECLARE CURSOR, DESCRIBE, EXECUTE,

EXECUTE IMMEDIATE, FETCH, OPEN, PREPARE, or SELECT...
INTO. Also, you cannot prepare the INCLUDE or WHENEVER
directives.

■ You cannot include references to host variables in the prepared SQL
statement.

■ You can include parameter indicators—the question mark (?) in
most implementations—in the *host-variable* string to denote values
that are to be substituted when the prepared statement is referenced
in an OPEN or EXECUTE statement. You can use a parameter indicator wherever a numeric literal, string literal, or host variable is
allowed in the SQL statement, but you cannot use a parameter indicator as a table, view, or column name.

■ You can reference any prepared statement in a DESCRIBE statement. You can refer only to a prepared SELECT statement in a
dynamic DECLARE CURSOR statement. You cannot reference a
prepared SELECT statement in an EXECUTE statement.

■ The system destroys any prepared statement definitions when an
application program terminates or a COMMIT WORK is executed.

## Example:

In a COBOL program, to dynamically prepare and execute an INSERT
statement that inserts rows into a table using values dynamically
retrieved from another table, enter the following:

```
WORKING-STORAGE SECTION.
  :
EXEC SQL
INCLUDE SQLDA END-EXEC.
  :
EXEC SQL
BEGIN DECLARE SECTION END-EXEC.
 01  DYNAMIC-STATEMENT   PIC X(250) VALUE
-      'SELECT CUSTNAME, ADDRESS
-        'FROM CUSTOMER
-        'WHERE FIRSTDATE = ?
-        'ORDER BY ZIP ASC'.
 01  SELECT-DATE           PIC 9999.
 01  DYNAMIC-INSERT        PIC X(150) VALUE
-      'INSERT INTO TEMPCUST VALUES (?,?)'.
EXEC SQL
END DECLARE SECTION END-EXEC.
  :
PROCEDURE DIVISION.
  :
```

```
*    (prepare the SELECT statement)
     EXEC SQL
     PREPARE CUST-SEARCH FROM :DYNAMIC-SELECT END-EXEC.
*    (describe the SELECT statement output)
     EXEC SQL
     DESCRIBE CUST-SEARCH INTO :SQLDA END-EXEC.
*    (prepare the INSERT statement)
     EXEC SQL
     PREPARE ISRT-CUST FROM :DYNAMIC-INSERT END-EXEC.
*    (declare a cursor on the SELECT statement)
     EXEC SQL
     DECLARE NEWCUST CURSOR FOR CUST-SEARCH END-EXEC.
*    (fetch rows, dynamically execute the INSERT statement)
     MOVE '1988' TO SELECT-DATE.
     EXEC SQL
     OPEN NEWCUST USING :SELECT-DATE END-EXEC.
     EXEC SQL
     WHENEVER NOT FOUND GO TO :DONE END-EXEC.
LOOP.
     EXEC SQL
     FETCH NEWCUST USING DESCRIPTOR :SQLDA END-EXEC.
     EXEC SQL
     EXECUTE ISRT-CUST USING DESCRIPTOR :SQLDA END-EXEC.
     GO TO LOOP.
DONE.
     EXEC SQL
     CLOSE NEWCUST END-EXEC.
```

**Note:** The statement INCLUDE SQLDA is not supported for COBOL
in every SQL implementation. The above example assumes that the
INCLUDE directive creates a data structure named SQLDA. Some implementations of the INCLUDE directive allow you to provide a name
for the SQLDA structure generated by the INCLUDE directive. See
your product documentation for details.

In a C program, to dynamically prepare and execute an INSERT statement that inserts rows into a table using values dynamically retrieved
from another table (also shown in the COBOL example), enter the
following:

```
EXEC SQL
INCLUDE SQLDA;
⋮
EXEC SQL
BEGIN DECLARE SECTION;
char *dynamic_statement =
   "SELECT CUSTNAME, ADDRESS \
    FROM CUSTOMER \
    WHERE FIRSTDATE = ? \
    ORDER BY ZIP ASC";
```

*(continued)*

```
char *select_date;
char *dynamic_insert =
  "INSERT INTO TEMPCUST VALUES (?,?)";
EXEC SQL
END DECLARE SECTION;
   :
/* prepare the SELECT statement */
EXEC SQL
PREPARE CUST_SEARCH FROM :dynamic_select;
   :
/* describe the SELECT statement output */
EXEC SQL
DESCRIBE CUST_SEARCH INTO :SQLDA;
/* prepare the INSERT statement */
EXEC SQL
PREPARE ISRT_CUST FROM :dynamic_insert;
   :
/* declare a cursor on the SELECT statement */
EXEC SQL
DECLARE NEWCUST CURSOR FOR CUST_SEARCH;
   :
/* fetch rows, dynamically execute the INSERT statement */
select_date = "1988";
EXEC SQL
OPEN NEWCUST USING :select_date;
EXEC SQL
WHENEVER NOT FOUND GO TO :DONE;
for (i = 1; i > 0; i++)
  {
  EXEC SQL
  FETCH NEWCUST USING DESCRIPTOR :SQLDA;
  EXEC SQL
  EXECUTE ISRT_CUST USING DESCRIPTOR :SQLDA;
  }
DONE.
EXEC SQL
CLOSE NEWCUST;
```

## See Also:

CLOSE Statement, DECLARE CURSOR Statement (Dynamic SQL),
DESCRIBE Statement (Dynamic SQL), EXECUTE Statement (Dynamic
SQL), FETCH Statement (Dynamic SQL), INCLUDE Directive, INSERT
Statement, and OPEN Statement (Dynamic SQL).

# Search-condition

## Syntax:

[NOT] {*predicate* ¦ (*search-condition*)}
  [{AND ¦ OR} [NOT] {*predicate* ¦ (*search-condition*)}]...

## Description:

Describes a simple or compound predicate that is true, false, or
unknown about a given row or group. Use a *search-condition* in the
WHERE clause of a SELECT statement, subSELECT clause, DELETE
statement, or UPDATE statement. It can also be used within the
HAVING clause in a SELECT statement. The *search-condition* defines
the rows that should appear in the resulting logical table or the rows
that should be acted upon by the change operation. If the *search-
condition* is true when applied to a row, that row is included in the
result table.

## Notes:

- The system effectively applies any subSELECT clause in the
  *search-condition* to each row of the table that is the result of the
  previous clauses. The system then evaluates the result of the
  subSELECT clause with regard to each candidate row.

- If you include a comparison predicate in the form *expression
  comparison-operator subselect-clause*, an error is returned if the
  subSELECT clause returns no rows.

- The order of evaluation of the Boolean operators is NOT, AND, and
  then OR. You can include additional parentheses to influence the
  order in which the Boolean expressions are processed.

- When using the Boolean operator NOT, the following holds: NOT
  (true) is false, NOT (false) is true, and NOT (unknown) is unknown.
  The result is unknown whenever a predicate references a NULL
  value. If a *search-condition* evaluates to false or unknown when applied to a row, the row is not selected. The system returns true,
  false, or unknown values as a result of applying AND or OR against
  two predicates or *search-conditions* according to the table on the
  next page.

| AND | true | false | unknown |
|---------|---------|-------|---------|
| true | true | false | unknown |
| false | false | false | false |
| unknown | unknown | false | unknown |

| OR | true | false | unknown |
|---------|------|---------|---------|
| true | true | true | true |
| false | true | false | unknown |
| unknown | true | unknown | unknown |

## Example:

To find all entries in the ACCTSPAY table for payee Acme Mail Order Company in which a check has been issued and has cleared the bank, enter the following:

```
SELECT *
  FROM ACCTSPAY
  WHERE PAYEENAME = 'Acme Mail Order Company'
    AND CHECKNUM IS NOT NULL
    AND CHECKNUM IN (SELECT CHECKNUM FROM CHECKLEDGER
      WHERE CHECKSTATUS = 'cleared');
```

## See Also:

DELETE Statement, Expressions, HAVING Clause, Predicates, SELECT Statement, subSELECT Clause, UPDATE Statement, and WHERE Clause.

# SELECT Statement

## Syntax:

SELECT [ALL ¦ DISTINCT] *select-list*
  FROM {{*table-name* ¦ *view-name*} [*correlation-name*]},...
  [WHERE *search-condition*]
  [GROUP BY {*column-name* ¦ *column-number*},...]
  [HAVING *search-condition*]
  [{INTERSECT ¦ MINUS ¦ UNION [ALL]} *select-statement*]
  [[ORDER BY {{*column-name* ¦ *column-number*} [ASC ¦ DESC]},...]
  [FOR UPDATE OF {*column-name*},...]]

*select-list* is: { * ¦ {*expression* ¦
                   *table-name*.* ¦
                   *view-name*.* ¦
                   *correlation-name*.* },... }

## Description:

Performs the relational operations select, project, and join to create a logical table from other tables or views. The items in the *select-list* identify the columns to be projected from one table to the table being formed. You identify the tables to be joined in the FROM clause, and you identify the join criteria as well as the rows to be selected in the WHERE clause. The DISTINCT keyword indicates that if identical rows exist, only one will be included.

## Notes:

■ You can execute this statement interactively or embed it in an application program as part of a DECLARE CURSOR or an INSERT INTO statement.

■ You can optionally supply a *correlation-name* for each *table-name* or *view-name* in the FROM clause. You can use this *correlation-name* as an alias for the full table name when qualifying *column-names* in the select list or the WHERE clause and subclauses. If you are joining a table or view to itself, you need *correlation-names* to indicate the copy of the table or view to which you are referring in the *select-list*, join criteria, or selection criteria.

■ If you specify more than one table or view in the FROM clause of a SELECT statement or subSELECT clause, the SQL system logically creates the Cartesian product of all the tables or views. (See the Joins section for explanation and examples of the Cartesian product.) The system then returns the rows in which the selection and join criteria specified in the WHERE clause are true.

■ Refer to your product documentation for rules on the formation of legal *table-names* or *view-names*.

■ A *column-name* in a GROUP BY clause can refer to any column from any table in the FROM clause, even if the column is not named in the *select-list*.

■ Use a *column-number* in the GROUP BY clause to reference an unnamed column (such as an *expression*) in the *select-list*.

■ If the GROUP BY clause is preceded by a WHERE clause, the system forms the groups from the rows selected after application of the WHERE clause. In some implementations, the sequence in which you specify the WHERE and GROUP BY clauses is significant.

■ When you include a GROUP BY clause, the *select-list* must be made up of either column functions (AVG, COUNT, MAX, MIN, or SUM) or *column-names* specified in the GROUP BY clause.

- In most implementations, you cannot use a GROUP BY or HAVING clause in a SELECT statement or subSELECT clause if the SELECT statement or subSELECT clause contains a FROM clause that references a view that is defined using a GROUP BY or HAVING clause.

- If you use a HAVING clause but do not include a GROUP BY clause, the *select-list* must be formed using column functions (AVG, COUNT, MAX, MIN, or SUM).

- If you include a GROUP BY clause preceding the HAVING clause, the HAVING *search-condition* applies to each of the groups formed by like values in the specified columns. If you do not include a GROUP BY clause, the HAVING *search-condition* applies to the entire logical table defined by the SELECT statement.

- In some implementations, the system applies the HAVING clause to the results of the immediately preceding clauses. This means

  SELECT ... WHERE ... HAVING ... GROUP BY ...

  is processed differently than

  SELECT ... WHERE ... GROUP BY ... HAVING ...

  In other implementations, the system always applies the HAVING clause to the results of any GROUP BY clause regardless of the order of the clauses. Consult your product documentation for details.

- A *column-name* in the ORDER BY clause can be ambiguous because the same name might appear in a *select-list* more than once, or because different column names might appear in the same position through an INTERSECT, a MINUS, or a UNION operation, which causes the column names in the result table to be undefined. If the *column-name* is ambiguous, you must specify a relative *column-number* in the ORDER BY clause.

- You can specify multiple columns in the ORDER BY clause. The list is ordered primarily by the first *column-name* or *column-number*. If there are rows in which the values of that column are equal, they are then ordered by the next *column-name* or *column-number* on the ORDER BY list.

- You can specify ascending (ASC) or descending (DESC) ordering for each column. If you choose neither ASC nor DESC, ASC is assumed.

- Unless you use an ORDER BY clause in a SELECT statement, the sequence of the returned rows is undefined in most implementations.

## Examples:

In a COBOL program, to declare a logical table that includes only customers who first did business in 1988 and that lists them in ascending order by zip code, enter the following:

```
EXEC SQL
DECLARE NEWCUST CURSOR FOR
  SELECT CUSTNAME, ADDRESS FROM CUSTOMER
    WHERE FIRSDATE = '1988'
    ORDER BY ZIP ASC END-EXEC.
```

In a C program, to declare a logical table that includes all payments owed to the Acme Mail Order Company and that allows the check number to be inserted, enter the following:

```
EXEC SQL
DECLARE ACMEOWE CURSOR FOR
  SELECT PAYEENAME, ADDRESS, AMTOWED, CHECKNUM
    FROM ACCTSPAY
    WHERE PAYEENAME = 'Acme Mail Order Company'
    FOR UPDATE OF CHECKNUM;
```

To find the average amount owed to any vendor who sent a bill in October, enter the following:

```
SELECT AVG(AMTOWED)
  FROM ACCTSPAY
  WHERE MOBILL = 10
    AND AMTOWED > 0;
```

To find the number of different prices for items in the current inventory, enter the following:

```
SELECT COUNT(DISTINCT COST)
  FROM INVENTORY
  WHERE QTY > 0;
```

To select information about customers and their purchases over $10, enter the following:

```
SELECT A.CUSTNO, A.CUSTNAME, A.ADDRESS,
 B.PURCHDATE, B.PURCHAMT, B.ITEMNO,
 C.ITEMNAME
  FROM CUSTOMER A, PURCHASE B, ITEMMAST C
  WHERE A.CUSTNO = B.CUSTNO
    AND B.ITEMNO = C.ITEMNO
    AND B.PURCHAMT > 10;
```

To find the largest purchase from each group (categorized by zip code) whose largest purchase is less than the average of purchases from all customers, enter the following:

```
SELECT ZIP, MAX(PURCHAMT)
  FROM CUSTOMER A, PURCHASE B
  WHERE A.CUSTNO = B.CUSTNO
  GROUP BY ZIP
  HAVING MAX(PURCAMT) <
    (SELECT AVG(PURCAMT) FROM PURCHASE);
```

To find the average and maximum amounts owed to suppliers in the state of Texas every month that the maximum amount owed is under $1,000, enter the following:

```
SELECT MOBILL, AVG(AMTOWED), MAX(AMTOWED)
  FROM SUPPLIER S, ACCTSPAY A
  WHERE S.SUPPNO = A.ACCTNO
    AND S.STATE = 'TX'
  GROUP BY MONTH
  HAVING MAX(AMTOWED) < 1000;
```

To move from the table CUSTOMER and insert into a temporary table names of customers who live in the state of Oregon, enter the following:

```
INSERT INTO TEMPCUST
  SELECT CUSTNAME, ADDRESS FROM CUSTOMER
    WHERE STATE = 'OR';
```

To find all suppliers and customers in the state of Massachusetts and sort them by zip code, enter the following:

```
SELECT CUSTNAME, ZIP
  FROM CUSTOMER WHERE STATE = 'MA'
UNION
SELECT SUPPNAME, ZIP
  FROM SUPPLIER WHERE STATE = 'MA'
ORDER BY 2;
```

### See Also:

DECLARE CURSOR Statement, INSERT Statement, INTERSECT Query Operator, Joins, MINUS Query Operator, Search-condition, and UNION Query Operator.

# SELECT...INTO Statement

### Syntax:

SELECT [ALL ¦ DISTINCT] *select-list*
  INTO {:*host-variable*},...

*(continued)*

```
FROM {{table-name ¦ view-name} [correlation-name]},...
[WHERE search-condition]
[GROUP BY {column-name ¦ column-number},...]
[HAVING search-condition]
```

*select-list* is: {* ¦ {*expression* ¦
                        *table-name*.* ¦
                        *view-name*.* ¦
                        *correlation-name*.*},...}

## Description:

Creates a logical table of one row (at most) and assigns the values in that row to the specified host variables.

## Notes:

■ Only use this statement embedded in an application program. You must precede this statement with the EXEC SQL statement prefix and follow it with the SQL statement terminator appropriate to the application language. (See END-EXEC Statement Terminator.)

■ If more than one row exists in the result table, the system returns an error. If the result table is empty, the system returns an SQLCODE of 100.

■ The attributes of the receiving host variables must match the attributes of the columns returned. In addition, the number of host variables in the INTO clause must match the number of variables found in the *select-list*.

■ You can optionally supply a *correlation-name* for each *table-name* or *view-name* in the FROM clause. You can use this *correlation-name* as an alias for the full table name when you qualify *column-names* in the *select-list* or in the WHERE clause and subclauses. If you want to join a table or view to itself, you can use a *correlation-name* in the *select-list*, join criteria, or selection criteria to indicate the copy of the table or view.

■ If you specify more than one table or view in the FROM clause of the SELECT statement or subSELECT clause, the SQL system logically creates the Cartesian product of all of the tables or views. (See the Joins section for explanation and examples of the Cartesian product.) The system then returns the rows in which the selection and join criteria specified in the WHERE clause are true.

■ Refer to your product documentation for rules on the formation of legal *table-names* or *view-names*.

■ A *column-name* in a GROUP BY clause can refer to any column from any table in the FROM clause, even if the column is not named in the *select-list*.

- Use a *column-number* in the GROUP BY clause to reference an un-named column in the *select-list*, such as an *expression*.

- If a WHERE clause precedes the GROUP BY clause, the system forms groups from the selected rows after application of the WHERE clause. In some implementations, the sequence in which you specify the WHERE and GROUP BY clauses is significant.

- When you include a GROUP BY clause, the *select-list* must be made up of either column functions (AVG, COUNT, MAX, MIN, or SUM) or *column-names* specified in the GROUP BY clause.

- In most implementations, you cannot use the GROUP BY or HAVING clauses in a SELECT statement or subSELECT clause if the SELECT statement or subSELECT clause contains a FROM clause that references a view that is defined using a GROUP BY or HAVING clause.

- If you use a HAVING clause but do not include a GROUP BY clause, the *select-list* must be formed using column functions (AVG, COUNT, MAX, MIN, or SUM).

- If a GROUP BY clause precedes a HAVING clause, the HAVING *search-condition* applies to each of the groups formed by like values in the grouping columns. If you do not include a GROUP BY clause, the HAVING *search-condition* applies to the entire logical table de-fined by the SELECT statement.

- In some implementations, the system applies the HAVING clause to the results of the immediately preceding clauses. This means

  SELECT ...WHERE ... HAVING ... GROUP BY ...

  is processed differently than

  SELECT ...WHERE ... GROUP BY ... HAVING ...

  In other implementations, the system always applies the HAVING clause to the results of any GROUP BY clause regardless of the order of the clauses. Consult your product documentation for details.

## Examples:

In a COBOL program, to retrieve the average amount owed to vendors who sent a bill in October, enter the following:

```
EXEC SQL
SELECT AVG(AMTOWED)
  INTO :AVERAGE
  FROM ACCTSPAY
  WHERE MOBILL = 10
  AND AMTOWED > 0 END-EXEC.
```

In a C program, to retrieve the number of different prices for items in the current inventory, enter the following:

```
EXEC SQL
SELECT COUNT(DISTINCT COST)
  INTO :count_price
  FROM INVENTORY
  WHERE QTY > 0;
```

In a COBOL program, to retrieve information about customer number 5369 concerning a purchase made on September 4, 1982, enter the following:

```
EXEC SQL
SELECT A.CUSTNO, A.CUSTNAME, A.ADDRESS,
 B.PURCHDATE, B.PURCHAMT, B.ITEMNO,
 C.ITEMNAME
  INTO :NUMBER, :NAME, :ADDRESS, :DATE, :AMOUNT,
   :INUMBER, :INAME
  FROM CUSTOMER A, PURCHASE B, ITEMMAST C
  WHERE A.CUSTNO = B.CUSTNO
   AND B.ITEMNO = C.ITEMNO
   AND A.CUSTNO = 5369
   AND B.PURCHDATE = 090482 END-EXEC.
```

**See Also:**

Joins and Search-condition.

# subSELECT Clause

## Syntax:

(SELECT [ALL ¦ DISTINCT] *select-list*
   FROM {{*table-name* ¦ *view-name*} [*correlation-name*]},...
   [WHERE *search-condition*]
   [GROUP BY {*column-name* ¦ *column-number*},...]
   [HAVING *search-condition*])

*select-list* is: {∗ ¦ {*expression* ¦
              *table-name*.∗ ¦
              *view-name*.∗ ¦
              *correlation-name*.∗},... }

## Description:

Selects from a single column any number of values or no values at all for comparison in a predicate.

# Notes:

■ You can use the special character asterisk (*) in the *select-list* of a subSELECT clause only when the subSELECT clause is used in an EXISTS predicate, or when the FROM clause within the subSELECT clause refers to a single table or view that contains only one column.

■ In the *search-condition* of the WHERE clause of a subSELECT clause, you can refer via an outer reference to the columns of any table or view that is defined in the outer queries. You must qualify the *column-name* if the table or view reference is ambiguous.

■ You can optionally supply a *correlation-name* for each *table-name* or *view-name* in the FROM clause. You can use this *correlation-name* as an alias for the full table name when you qualify *column-names* in the WHERE clause and subclauses. If you want to join a table or a view to itself, you can use a *correlation-name* in the *select-list*, join criteria, or selection criteria to indicate the copy of the table or view.

■ If you specify more than one table or view in the FROM clause of a subSELECT clause, the SQL system logically creates the Cartesian product of all of the tables or views. (See the Joins section for explanation and examples of the Cartesian product.) The system then returns the rows in which the selection and join criteria specified in the WHERE clause are true.

■ Refer to your product documentation for rules on the formation of legal *table-names* or *view-names*.

■ A *column-name* in a GROUP BY clause can refer to any column from any table in the FROM clause, even if the column is not named in the *select-list*.

■ Use a *column-number* in the GROUP BY clause to reference an unnamed column (such as an *expression*) in the *select-list*.

■ If a WHERE clause precedes the GROUP BY clause, the system forms groups from the selected rows after the application of the WHERE clause. In some implementations, the sequence in which you specify the WHERE and GROUP BY clauses is significant.

■ When you include a GROUP BY or HAVING clause, the *select-list* must be made up of either column functions (AVG, COUNT, MAX, MIN, or SUM) or *column-names* specified in the GROUP BY clause.

■ In most implementations, you cannot use a GROUP BY or HAVING clause in a SELECT statement or subSELECT clause if the SELECT statement or subSELECT clause contains a FROM clause that references a view that is defined using a GROUP BY or HAVING clause.

- If a GROUP BY clause precedes a HAVING clause, the HAVING clause's *search-condition* applies to each of the groups formed by like values in the specified columns. If you do not include a GROUP BY clause, the HAVING clause's *search-condition* applies to the entire logical table defined by the SELECT statement.

- In some implementations, the system applies the HAVING clause to the results of the immediately preceding clauses. This means

  SELECT ... WHERE ... HAVING ... GROUP BY ...

  is processed differently than

  SELECT ... WHERE ... GROUP BY ... HAVING ...

  In other implementations, the system always applies the HAVING clause to the results of any GROUP BY clause regardless of the order of the clauses. Consult your product documentation for details.

## Examples:

To delete all rows in ACCTSPAY in which a check has been issued and has cleared the bank, enter the following:

```
DELETE FROM ACCTSPAY
  WHERE CHECKNUM NOT = NULL
    AND CHECKNUM IN (SELECT CHECKNUM FROM CHECKLEDGR
      WHERE CHECKSTATUS = 'cleared');
```

To find the largest purchase from each group (categorized by zip code) whose largest purchase is less than the average of all purchases from all customers, enter the following:

```
SELECT ZIP, MAX(PURCHAMT)
  FROM CUSTOMERS A, PURCHASE B
  WHERE A.CUSTNO = B.CUSTNO
  GROUP BY ZIP
  HAVING MAX(PURCHAMT) <
    (SELECT AVG(PURCHAMT) FROM PURCHASE);
```

To find the inventory item name and supplier name for any item that has an inventory cost of less than $50, enter the following:

```
SELECT ITEMNAME, SUPNAME
  FROM INVENTORY I, SUPPLIER S
  WHERE EXISTS
    (SELECT * FROM INVENTORY I2
      WHERE I.ITEMNO = I2.ITEMNO
        AND (I2.QTY * I2.COST) < 50);
```

**Note:** In the above example, the inner subSELECT clause makes an outer reference to the INVENTORY table in the SELECT statement by specifically referring to the correlation name 'I' (I.ITEMNO in the

WHERE clause of the subSELECT clause). The system is then forced to evaluate the subSELECT clause for every row in the SELECT statement, which might not be the most efficient way to achieve the desired result.

**See Also:**

Expressions and Predicates.

---

# UNION Query Operator

## Syntax:

*select-statement*
UNION [ALL]
*select-statement*
[ORDER BY {*integer* [ASC ¦ DESC]},...]

## Description:

Produces a result table that contains the rows returned by both the first *select-statement* and the second *select-statement*.

## Notes:

- If you specify ALL, the system returns all rows in both logical tables. If you do not specify ALL, the system eliminates duplicate rows.

- The tables returned by each SELECT statement must contain an equal number of columns, and each column must have identical attributes.

- You must not use the ORDER BY clause in the SELECT statements that are joined by query operators; however, you can include a single ORDER BY clause at the end of a statement that uses one or more query operators. This action will apply the specified order to the result of the entire statement.

- You cannot use the FOR UPDATE clause in a statement that includes a query operator.

- Column names in the result table are undefined. You can refer to result columns (for example, in an ORDER BY clause) by position number.

- Most implementations that support query operators (INTERSECT, MINUS, UNION) allow you to combine multiple *select-statements*

using these operators to obtain complex results. You can use parentheses to influence the sequence in which the system applies the
operators. For example,

SELECT ... UNION (SELECT ... INTERSECT SELECT ...)

## Example:

To find the names of all suppliers and customers in the state of
Massachusetts, to eliminate duplicates, and to sort the names by zip
code, enter the following:

```
SELECT CUSTNAME, ZIP
  FROM CUSTOMER WHERE STATE = 'MA'
UNION
SELECT SUPNAME, ZIP
  FROM SUPPLIER WHERE STATE = 'MA'
ORDER BY 2;
```

## See Also:

INTERSECT Query Operator, MINUS Query Operator, ORDER BY
Clause, and SELECT Statement.

---

# UPDATE Statement

## Syntax:

UPDATE {*table-name* ¦ *view-name*}
  SET {*column-name* = {*expression* ¦ NULL}},...
  [WHERE *search-condition*]

## Description:

In the specified table or view, updates the selected columns (either to
the value of the given expression or to NULL) in all rows that satisfy
the *search-condition*. If you do not enter a WHERE clause, all rows in
the specified table or view are affected.

## Notes:

■ You can embed this statement in an application program when you
  precede it with the required EXEC SQL statement prefix and follow
  it with the SQL statement terminator appropriate to the application
  language. (See END-EXEC Statement Terminator.)

- Some SQL implementations support only a *table-name* in the FROM clause. Generally, when a *view-name* is supported in the FROM clause, the view must be constructed from only one base table.

- If you specify a *search-condition*, you can reference only columns found in the target table or view. If you use a subSELECT clause in the *search-condition*, you must not reference the target table or view, or any underlying table of the view in the subSELECT clause.

- In the SET clause, you cannot qualify a column name, nor can you specify a column name more than once.

- Values assigned to columns must be compatible with the column attributes. If you assign the NULL value, the column cannot have been defined NOT NULL.

- Many systems provide the ability to define column-value constraints, editing routines, or referential integrity checks. Any values that you update must pass these validations before the system accepts the updated row.

- If you are updating a view that was declared using the WITH CHECK OPTION clause, the updated row must pass the view-selection criteria.

- If you are updating a view that does not include the WITH CHECK OPTION clause, the row must pass only the validation criteria of the underlying table; however, you cannot retrieve the updated row with the view if the row does not pass the view-selection criteria.

### Examples:

To update the amount owed in the ACCTSPAY table for account number 7859, enter the following:

```
UPDATE ACCTSPAY
  SET AMTOWED = 153.95
  WHERE ACCTNO = 7859;
```

To discount the price of all items in the item master, enter the following:

```
UPDATE ITEMMAST
  SET PRICE = PRICE * .95;
```

### See Also:

Expressions, Predicates, Search-conditions, and WHERE Clause.

# UPDATE...WHERE CURRENT OF Statement

## Syntax:

UPDATE {*table-name* ¦ *view-name*}
   SET {*column-name* = {*expression* ¦ NULL}},...
   WHERE CURRENT OF *cursor-name*

## Description:

Updates the selected columns (to either the value of *expression* or to NULL) in the specified table or view in the row currently pointed to by the specified cursor.

## Notes:

- Only use this statement embedded in an application program. You must precede this statement with the EXEC SQL statement prefix and follow it with the SQL statement terminator appropriate to the application language. (See END-EXEC Statement Terminator.)

- The *table-name* or *view-name* must be the same as the *table-name* or *view-name* used in the specified cursor.

- Some SQL implementations support only a *table-name* in the FROM clause. Generally, when a *view-name* is supported in the FROM clause, the view must be constructed from only one base table.

- In the SET clause, you cannot qualify a column name, nor can you specify a column name more than once.

- Values assigned to columns must be compatible with the column attributes. If you assign the NULL value, the column cannot have been defined NOT NULL.

- In the SET clause, you can use only columns that you named in the FOR UPDATE OF clause of the DECLARE CURSOR statement.

- Many systems provide the ability to define column-value constraints, editing routines, or referential integrity checks. Any values that you update must pass these validations before the system accepts the updated row.

- If you are updating a view that was declared using the WITH CHECK OPTION clause, the updated row must pass the view-selection criteria.

- If you are updating a view that does not include the WITH CHECK OPTION clause, the row must pass only the validation criteria of the underlying table; however, you cannot retrieve the updated row with the view if the row does not pass the view-selection criteria.

## Example:

In a COBOL program, to retrieve a logical table that includes all payments owed to the Acme Mail Order Company, and to update the check number, enter the following:

```
EXEC SQL
DECLARE ACMEOWE CURSOR FOR
SELECT PAYEENAME, ADDRESS, AMTOWED, CHECKNUM
   FROM ACCTSPAY
   WHERE PAYEENAME = 'Acme Mail Order Company'
   FOR UPDATE OF CHECKNUM END-EXEC.
   ⋮
EXEC SQL
OPEN CURSOR ACMEOWE END-EXEC.
⋮
EXEC SQL
FETCH CURSOR ACMEOWE INTO :NAME, :ADDRESS,
 :AMOUNT, :NUMBER END-EXEC.
MOVE 123 to NUMBER.
EXEC SQL
UPDATE ACCTSPAY
   SET CHECKNUM = :NUMBER
   WHERE CURRENT OF ACMEOWE END-EXEC.
```

In a C program, to retrieve a logical table that includes all customers, and to update the customer number in the row pointed to by the cursor, enter the following:

```
EXEC SQL
DECLARE NEW_CUST CURSOR FOR
   SELECT CUSTNAME, STATE
     FROM CUSTOMER
     FOR UPDATE OF STATE;
     ⋮
EXEC SQL
OPEN CURSOR NEW_CUST;
⋮
EXEC SQL
FETCH CURSOR NEW_CUST INTO :name, :newstate;
newstate = "TX";
EXEC SQL
UPDATE CUSTOMER
   SET STATE = :newstate;
   WHERE CURRENT OF NEW_CUST;
```

## See Also:

DECLARE CURSOR Statement, END-EXEC Statement Terminator, EXEC SQL Statement Prefix, Expressions, FETCH Statement, and OPEN Statement.

# WHENEVER Directive

## Syntax:

WHENEVER {NOT FOUND ¦ SQLERROR ¦ SQLWARNING}
  {CONTINUE ¦ GOTO *:host-label* ¦ GO TO *:host-label* ¦
  PERFORM *:host-label* ¦ CALL *:host-label*}

## Description:

Specifies action to be taken when certain SQL exception conditions are encountered. These conditions are: no rows found (NOT FOUND), SQL system error (SQLERROR), and SQL system warning (SQLWARNING).

## Notes:

■ Only use this statement embedded in an application program. You must precede this statement with the EXEC SQL statement prefix and follow it with the SQL statement terminator appropriate to the application language. (See END-EXEC Statement Terminator.)

■ A WHENEVER condition statement with no action clause sets (or resets if the WHENEVER statement had previously been called for that condition) the action clause for that condition to CONTINUE, which is the default action. No special operations are performed when the exception condition is met. If you want your program to perform a series of steps when the exception condition is met, you can specify an action clause. Some examples of action clauses are GOTO, GO TO, PERFORM, and CALL. The necessary SQL keyword depends on the host language and the implementation. Refer to your product documentation for details.

■ You can enter as many WHENEVER statements as are necessary to control the action taken on an exception condition for each SQL statement in your program. The scope of a WHENEVER statement includes all SQL statements in your program up to the point at which another WHENEVER statement for the same condition is found in the source code by the precompiler. The scope of a WHENEVER directive is not related to the execution sequence of your program statements.

## Example:

In a COBOL program, to set up a condition check for defaulting to the ABORT routine when an error occurs, going to EOF when the "not found" condition is met, and ignoring all warnings returned to the program, enter the following:

```
EXEC SQL
WHENEVER SQLERROR GO TO ABORT END-EXEC.
EXEC SQL
WHENEVER SQLWARNING CONTINUE END-EXEC.
EXEC SQL
WHENEVER NOT FOUND GO TO EOF END-EXEC.
```

In a C program, to set up a condition check for defaulting to the DONE routine when the "not found" condition is met, enter the following:

```
EXEC SQL
WHENEVER NOT FOUND GO TO DONE;
```

# WHERE Clause

## Syntax:

WHERE *search-condition*

## Description:

Specifies a *search-condition* in an SQL statement or clause. The DELETE, SELECT, or UPDATE statements, or the subSELECT clause containing the WHERE clause, operates only on those rows that satisfy the condition.

## Notes:

■ The system applies the *search-condition* to each row of the logical table assembled as a result of executing the previous clauses, and it rejects those rows for which the *search-condition* does not evaluate to true. If you use a subSELECT clause within a predicate in the *search-condition* (often called an inner query), the system must first execute the subSELECT clause before it evaluates the predicate.

■ In a subSELECT clause, if you refer to a table or view that you also use in an outer FROM clause (often called a correlated subquery), the system must execute the subSELECT clause for each row being evaluated in the outer table. If you do not use a reference to an outer table in a subSELECT clause, the system must execute the subSELECT clause only once. A correlated subquery can also be expressed as a join, which on many systems might execute more efficiently.

- If you include a predicate in the *search-condition* in the following form:

  *expression...comparison-operator...subselect-clause*

  an error is returned if the subSELECT clause returns no rows.

- The order of evaluation of the Boolean operators used in the *search-condition* is NOT, AND, and then OR. You can include additional parentheses to influence the order in which the system processes Boolean expressions.

## Example:

To find all entries in ACCTSPAY for payee Acme Mail Order Company in which a check has been issued and has cleared the bank, enter the following:

```
SELECT *
  FROM ACCTSPAY
  WHERE PAYEENAME = 'Acme Mail Order Company'
   AND CHECKNUM IS NOT NULL
   AND CHECKNUM IN (SELECT CHECKNUM FROM CHECKLEDGER
    WHERE CHECKSTATUS = 'cleared');
```

## See Also:

DELETE Statement, Expressions, Predicates, Search-condition, SELECT Statement, subSELECT Clause, and UPDATE Statement.

# *Data Definition Language*

---

## ALTER TABLE Statement

### Syntax:

ALTER TABLE *table-name* ADD COLUMN *column-name data-type*
  [NOT NULL] [DEFAULT {*literal* ¦ SYSTEM}]

ALTER TABLE *table-name* ADD (*column-name data-type*)
  [NOT NULL WITH DEFAULT]

ALTER TABLE *table-name* ADD *column-name data-type*
  [NULL ¦ NOT NULL]

### Description:

Adds a new column to an existing table.

### Notes:

- Because this statement is not part of the ANSI-86 SQL standard, several different variants exist. The most common syntax implementations are shown. Consult your product documentation for details.

- In general, execution of this statement locks a table and commits all pending changes.

- Most implementations logically insert the new column at the end of the existing table. The new column must either be allowed to contain the NULL value or have a default value assigned. In response to requests for values in the column, the system returns the NULL or default value until an actual value for the column is created in the table through an UPDATE or INSERT operation. If you specify a system default (NOT NULL DEFAULT SYSTEM or NOT NULL WITH DEFAULT), the system uses a value appropriate to the data type, such as zero for numeric fields and blank for character fields.

- You cannot use any view that exists prior to the execution of the ALTER TABLE to read the new column, even if the view is defined using SELECT *. You must drop and re-create the view to use the new column in the view.

## Example:

To add to the table CUSTOMER a column that contains an additional address, enter the following:

```
ALTER TABLE CUSTOMER ADD (ADDRESS2 CHAR(30));
```

## See Also:

CREATE TABLE Statement, CREATE VIEW Statement, DROP VIEW Statement, and Appendix (Common Data Types).

# COMMENT ON Statement

## Syntax:

COMMENT ON {COLUMN *column-name* ON {*table-name* ¦
*view-name*} ¦ INDEX *index-name* ¦ TABLE *table-name* ¦
VIEW *view-name* } IS *string-literal* [CLEAR]

COMMENT ON {TABLE *table-name* ¦ COLUMN
*table-name.column-name* }
  IS *string-literal*

COMMENT ON {{TABLE {*table-name* ¦ *view-name*} ¦
COLUMN {*table-name.column-name* ¦ *view-name.column-name*}
IS *string-literal*} ¦
{*table-name* ¦ *view-name*} ({*column-name* IS *string-literal*},...)}

## Description:

Adds or replaces comments about tables, views, columns, or indexes, in the system catalog. Use COMMENT ON to provide additional documentation about the SQL objects (tables, views, columns, or indexes) that you have created.

## Notes:

■ Because this statement is not part of the ANSI-86 SQL standard, several different variants exist. The most common syntax implementations are shown. Consult your product documentation for details.

■ Some implementations allow you to keep multiple lines of comments on objects. Others provide for only one comment per object, and any new comment that you supply takes the place of the previous comment. In all cases, providing an empty string literal (" " or ' ', depending on the implementation) erases all comments stored about the object.

- Some implementations allow the use of the CLEAR clause, which indicates that all comments that have been added to the given column, index, table, or view will be replaced with the *string-literal* of the COMMENT ON statement.

- You can access previously stored comments through a view defined on the system catalog. Consult your product documentation for details.

### Example:

To add a comment about the table CUSTOMER, enter the following:

```
COMMENT ON TABLE CUSTOMER
   IS 'This table contains information about customers.';
```

# CREATE INDEX Statement

### Syntax:

CREATE [UNIQUE] INDEX *index-name* ON *table-name*
  ({*column-name* [ASC ¦ DESC]},...)

### Description:

Creates an index of values for the specified columns of the target base table. The columns need not be contiguous within the table. The system uses indexes to decrease the time required to locate specific rows in the database.

### Notes:

- Although this statement is not part of the ANSI-86 SQL standard, most implementations accept the syntax shown. All implementations also have extensions for describing physical attributes of the index such as amount of disk space, free space, or compression, or for specifying index creation options. Consult your product documentation for details.

- You can embed this statement in an application program when you precede it with the required EXEC SQL statement prefix and follow it with the SQL statement terminator appropriate to the application language. (See END-EXEC Statement Terminator.) Note that execution of this statement can render your application invalid and make it necessary to recompile.

- If any other embedded statements in your program reference the table containing the newly created index, they must be recompiled before they are valid for execution again.

- If you embed this statement in an application program, any dynamic statements referencing the base table that you prepared subsequent to creating this index might not take advantage of this index until you have executed a COMMIT statement.

- The ordering of numeric columns is based strictly on numeric value. The ordering of alphanumeric columns depends on the internal character set supported by the system (ASCII or EBCDIC). Consult your product documentation for details.

- Indexes can decrease the amount of time required to access rows in the table but generally slow down UPDATE and INSERT operations because of the additional information that the system must maintain.

- If you use the UNIQUE option, two or more rows in the table cannot have indexed columns that contain the same value. If the system detects a duplicate value while building the index, the system usually will not build the index. Once a UNIQUE index exists, you cannot insert a new row or update an existing row if an index value is already in the table.

- Most systems make the table available for read-only access during index creation. If you are creating an index for a table that contains many rows, building the index entries can take a long time and adversely affect access to the table. Therefore, you should plan to build a large index only when access requirements are low and when updates to the table can be suspended while the index creation is in process.

## Example:

To build a new index for the CUSTOMER table zip-code column, enter the following:

```
CREATE INDEX CUSTZIP ON CUSTOMER (ZIP);
```

## See Also:

CREATE TABLE Statement, DROP TABLE Statement, UPDATE STATISTICS Statement, and COMMIT Statement (Data Control Language).

# CREATE SYNONYM Statement

## Syntax:

CREATE SYNONYM *synonym-name* FOR {*table-name* ¦ *view-name*}

## Description:

Creates an alias name for a table or view. Most systems require you to fully qualify the name of a table or view that is owned by another user with that user's identifier in the form *user-id.table-name*. A synonym can be useful to provide a shorthand name in place of a fully qualified *table-name* or *view-name*.

## Notes:

- Although this statement is not part of the ANSI-86 SQL standard, most implementations accept the syntax shown. In some implementations, the synonym is available only to you and must be unique within your user identifier. In other systems, a synonym can be declared public and shared with all users. Consult your product documentation for details.

- You can embed this statement in an application program when you precede it with the required EXEC SQL statement prefix and follow it with the SQL statement terminator appropriate to the application language. (See END-EXEC Statement Terminator.) Note that you cannot use this synonym in the program until you have executed a COMMIT statement.

## Example:

To create a synonym for the table PROD.CUSTOMER and use it in a SELECT statement, enter the following:

```
CREATE SYNONYM CUST FOR PROD.CUSTOMER;
SELECT * FROM CUST WHERE STATE = 'CO';
```

## See Also:

DROP SYNONYM Statement and COMMIT Statement (Data Control Language).

# CREATE TABLE Statement

## Syntax:

ANSI-86 standard:

CREATE TABLE *table-name*
({*column-name data-type* [NOT NULL [UNIQUE]] ¦
UNIQUE({*column-name*},...)},...)

Common implementation:

CREATE TABLE *table-name*
({*column-name data-type* [NOT NULL]},...)

## Description:

Creates a new table and defines the columns within the table.

## Notes:

- All implementations support the common syntax shown. Many
  implementations provide syntax for the definition of uniqueness
  constraints, but they do not all follow the ANSI standard. Most
  implementations provide additional syntax for describing the physical storage for the table, table partitioning, compression, default
  values, or validation criteria. Consult your product documentation
  for details.

- You can embed this statement in an application program when you
  precede it with the required EXEC SQL statement prefix and follow
  it with the SQL statement terminator appropriate to the application
  language. (See END-EXEC Statement Terminator.) Note that your
  program might not be able to access this new table until you have
  executed a COMMIT statement.

- Common data types include the following:
  CHAR[ACTER] (*length*)
  VARCHAR (*max-length*)
  NUMERIC (*precision*[,*scale*])
  DEC[IMAL] (*precision*[,*scale*])
  INT[EGER]
  SMALLINT
  FLOAT
  REAL
  DOUBLE PRECISION

  Refer to your product documentation for details.

## Example:

To create the table CUSTOMER, enter the following:

```
CREATE TABLE CUSTOMER
  (CUSTNO DECIMAL(5), CUSTNAME CHAR(25),
   ADDRESS CHAR(25), CITY CHAR(25),
   STATE CHAR(2), ZIP DECIMAL(5),
   FIRSDATE DECIMAL(6));
```

## See Also:

DROP TABLE Statement, COMMIT Statement (Data Control Language), and Appendix (Common Data Types).

# CREATE VIEW Statement

## Syntax:

CREATE VIEW *view-name* [({*view-column-name*},...)]
  AS *select-statement*
  [WITH CHECK OPTION]

## Description:

Creates a logical table that is derived by selecting a subset of the columns or rows from one or more tables or from other views.

## Notes:

■ You can embed this statement in an application program when you precede it with the required EXEC SQL statement prefix and follow it with the SQL statement terminator appropriate to the application language. (See END-EXEC Statement Terminator.) Note that you might not be able to reference this view in your program until you have executed a COMMIT statement.

■ If you do not include a *view-column-name* list, the columns in the view inherit names from the columns returned by the *select-statement*. If any column returned by the *select-statement* has the same name as that of another column or is derived from a column function, a constant, or an arithmetic expression, you must supply a *view-column-name* list and specify every column received in the view.

■ If you add a new column to an underlying table using ALTER TABLE, you must drop and re-create the view to use the new column in the view, even if you defined the view using SELECT *.

- Specify WITH CHECK OPTION if you have defined an updatable view by using the FOR UPDATE OF clause in the *select-statement* and if you want the system to validate against the selection criteria in the SELECT statement any row updated or inserted through the view. If you do not specify WITH CHECK OPTION, it is possible to update or insert a row in the view and then not be able to retrieve it through the view.

- You cannot update a view that you create by using a SELECT statement with an ORDER BY clause or with any query operator (INTERSECT, MINUS, or UNION).

- You cannot update a view created with a SELECT statement that includes a column function, the DISTINCT keyword, the GROUP BY or HAVING clauses, or a subSELECT statement that references the same base table as the SELECT statement.

- You cannot update a view declared with a SELECT statement that references more than one table or a read-only view in the FROM clause.

- With some implementations, you cannot use a query operator (INTERSECT, MINUS, or UNION) to define a view.

## Examples:

To create a view called NYCUST that contains only rows from the table CUSTOMER for customers in the state of New York and that checks all updates and inserts, enter the following:

```
CREATE VIEW NYCUST
  AS SELECT * FROM CUSTOMER
    WHERE STATE = 'NY'
  WITH CHECK OPTION;
```

To create a view containing information about customers and their purchases over $10, enter the following:

```
CREATE VIEW CUSTINFO
  (NUMBER, NAME, ADDR, DATE, AMOUNT, ITEMNO, ITEMNAME)
  AS SELECT A.CUSTNO, A.CUSTNAME, A.ADDRESS,
    B.PURCHDATE, B.PURCHAMT, B.ITEMNO,
    C.ITEMNAME
    FROM CUSTOMER A, PURCHASE B, ITEMMAST C
    WHERE A.CUSTNO = B.CUSTNO
      AND B.ITEMNO = C.ITEMNO
      AND B.PURCHAMT > 10;
```

## See Also:

SELECT Statement (Data Manipulation Language), CREATE TABLE Statement, DROP VIEW Statement, and COMMIT Statement (Data Control Language).

# DROP INDEX Statement

**Syntax:**

DROP INDEX *index-name*

**Description:**

Removes an index and releases any space occupied by the index.

**Notes:**

- Although this statement is not part of the ANSI-86 SQL standard, all implementations accept the syntax shown.

- You can embed this statement in an application program when you precede it with the required EXEC SQL statement prefix and follow it with the SQL statement terminator appropriate to the application language. (See END-EXEC Statement Terminator.) Note that execution of this statement can render your application invalid and make it necessary to recompile if any other embedded statements in your program reference the table containing the dropped index.

- The system renders invalid any views or applications that reference the dropped index. You should recompile any affected application programs or rebuild any affected views after the index is dropped.

**Example:**

To drop the CUSTZIP index that was built on the table CUSTOMER, enter the following:

```
DROP INDEX CUSTZIP;
```

**See Also:**

CREATE INDEX Statement.


# DROP SYNONYM Statement

**Syntax:**

DROP SYNONYM *synonym-name*

## Description:

Removes a synonym.

## Notes:

■ Although this statement is not part of the ANSI-86 SQL standard, all implementations that support synonyms accept the syntax shown. Consult your product documentation for details.

■ You can embed this statement in an application program when you precede it with the required EXEC SQL statement prefix and follow it with the SQL statement terminator appropriate to the application language. (See END-EXEC Statement Terminator.) Note that execution of this statement can render your application invalid and make it necessary to recompile if any other embedded statements in your program reference the dropped synonym.

■ The system renders invalid any views or application plans that reference the dropped synonym. You should recompile any affected application programs or rebuild any affected views after the synonym is dropped.

## Example:

To drop the CUST synonym, enter the following:

```
DROP SYNONYM CUST;
```

## See Also:

CREATE SYNONYM Statement.

# DROP TABLE Statement

## Syntax:

DROP TABLE *table-name*

## Description:

Removes a table and all indexes on the table and releases all space occupied by the table and its indexes.

## Notes:

■ Although this statement is not part of the ANSI-86 SQL standard, all implementations accept the syntax shown.

- You can embed this statement in an application program when you precede it with the required EXEC SQL statement prefix and follow it with the SQL statement terminator appropriate to the application language. (See END-EXEC Statement Terminator.) Note that execution of this statement can render your application invalid and make it necessary to recompile if any other embedded statements in your program reference the dropped table.

- The system renders invalid any views or applications that reference the dropped table. You should recompile any affected application programs or rebuild any affected views after the table is dropped.

## Example:

To drop the table CUSTOMER, enter the following:

```
DROP TABLE CUSTOMER;
```

## See Also:

CREATE TABLE Statement.

# DROP VIEW Statement

## Syntax:

DROP VIEW *view-name*

## Description:

Removes a view.

## Notes:

- Although this statement is not part of the ANSI-86 SQL standard, all implementations accept the syntax shown.

- You can embed this statement in an application program when you precede it with the required EXEC SQL statement prefix and follow it with the SQL statement terminator appropriate to the application language. (See END-EXEC Statement Terminator.) However, execution of this statement can render your application invalid and make it necessary to recompile if any other embedded statements in your program reference the dropped view.

- The system renders invalid any views or applications that reference the dropped view. You should recompile any affected application programs or rebuild any affected views after the view is dropped.

## Example:

To drop the CUSTINFO view, enter the following:

```
DROP VIEW CUSTINFO;
```

## See Also:

CREATE VIEW Statement.

# UPDATE STATISTICS Statement

## Syntax:

UPDATE [ALL] STATISTICS FOR TABLE *table-name*

## Description:

Updates statistics in the system catalog about the count and distribution of values in the indexes on the specified table. The query optimizer uses these statistics to determine an optimal access path for any query.

## Notes:

■ Because this statement is not part of the ANSI-86 SQL standard, several different variants exist. One of the most common syntax implementations is shown. Consult your product documentation for details.

■ In general, execution of this statement locks the table and commits all pending changes.

■ Some systems render invalid any views or applications that reference a table that has had its statistics updated. You should recompile any affected application programs or rebuild any affected views after statistics are updated.

## Example:

To update the statistics on the table CUSTOMER, enter the following:

```
UPDATE ALL STATISTICS FOR TABLE CUSTOMER;
```

## See Also:

CREATE INDEX Statement and DROP TABLE Statement.

# Data Control Language

## COMMIT Statement

### Syntax:

COMMIT [WORK]

### Description:

Commits changes made to database tables since the initiation of the application program or start of the interactive session, or since the last committing statement.

### Notes:

- You can embed this statement in an application program when you precede it with the required EXEC SQL statement prefix and follow it with the SQL statement terminator appropriate to the application language. (See END-EXEC Statement Terminator.)

- The system releases all locks.

- The system closes all open cursors, destroys any prepared statements, and renders invalid any cursors that you had associated with a prepared statement.

- You can use a ROLLBACK statement to reverse any changes made until you execute a COMMIT statement. Note that many data-definition commands automatically commit all work done to the point of the execution of the command.

### Example:

In a COBOL program, to commit all changes made since the last committing statement, enter the following:

```
EXEC SQL
COMMIT WORK END-EXEC.
```

In a C program, to commit all changes made since the last committing statement, enter the following:

```
EXEC SQL
COMMIT WORK;
```

**See Also:**

LOCK TABLE Statement and ROLLBACK Statement.

# GRANT Statement

## Syntax:

GRANT {ALL ¦ ALL PRIVILEGES ¦
{ALTER ¦ DELETE ¦ INDEX ¦ INSERT ¦ SELECT
¦ UPDATE[({*column-name*},...)]},... }
  ON {*table-name*},...
  TO {*user-id* ¦ PUBLIC},...
  [WITH GRANT OPTION]

## Description:

Grants privileges to users.

## Notes:

- You can embed this statement in an application program when you precede it with the required EXEC SQL statement prefix and follow it with the SQL statement terminator appropriate to the application language. (See END-EXEC Statement Terminator.)

- ALL or ALL PRIVILEGES implies the granting of all privileges that you own on the named table(s) to the users you specify.

- Use ALTER, DELETE, INSERT, SELECT, or UPDATE as keywords to grant the use of the corresponding statements. Use INDEX to grant use of the CREATE INDEX statement. You can restrict which columns can be updated by including a *column-name* list after the keyword UPDATE.

- PUBLIC grants these privileges to all users.

- WITH GRANT OPTION delegates to the users listed in the TO clause the right to grant the specified privileges to other users. You cannot use the WITH GRANT OPTION when you include PUBLIC in the *user-id* list.

## Example:

To grant to user identifiers JOHNDOE and JANEDOE both SELECT and UPDATE access to the table CUSTOMER and allow them to grant these privileges to others, enter the following:

```
GRANT SELECT, UPDATE
  ON CUSTOMER
  TO JOHNDOE, JANEDOE
  WITH GRANT OPTION;
```

## See Also:

REVOKE Statement.

# LOCK TABLE Statement

## Syntax:

LOCK TABLE {table-name : *view-name*}
  IN {SHARE : EXCLUSIVE} MODE

## Description:

Locks an entire table to restrict access by other users or transactions.

## Notes:

- Although this statement is not part of the ANSI-86 SQL standard, all implementations accept the syntax shown.

- You can embed this statement in an application program when you precede it with the required EXEC SQL statement prefix and follow it with the SQL statement terminator appropriate to the application language. (See END-EXEC Statement Terminator.)

- Locking in SHARE MODE allows other users to read but not to delete, update, or insert any rows in the table. You can still acquire EXCLUSIVE locks on some rows through execution of DELETE, INSERT, or UPDATE statements.

- Locking in EXCLUSIVE MODE disallows all other access to the table or any of its indexes. Use of this lock can have significant impact on the performance of other transactions that must wait for access to the table or index, particularly if you hold this lock for an extended period of time.

- The system releases all locks when your transaction or program ends or when you execute a COMMIT or ROLLBACK statement.

## Example:

To acquire a lock preventing other users from updating the table CUSTOMER, enter the following:

```
LOCK TABLE CUSTOMER IN SHARE MODE;
```

## See Also:

COMMIT Statement and ROLLBACK Statement.

# REVOKE Statement

## Syntax:

REVOKE {ALL ¦ ALL PRIVILEGES ¦
{ALTER ¦ DELETE ¦ INDEX ¦ INSERT ¦
SELECT ¦ UPDATE},... }
  ON {*table-name*},...
  FROM {*user-id* ¦ PUBLIC},...

## Description:

Revokes privileges from users.

## Notes:

■ Because this statement is not part of the ANSI-86 SQL standard, several different variants exist. Shown is one of the most common syntax implementations. Consult your product documentation for details.

■ You can embed this statement in an application program when you precede it with the required EXEC SQL statement prefix and follow it with the SQL statement terminator appropriate to the application language. (See END-EXEC Statement Terminator.)

■ ALL or ALL PRIVILEGES implies the removal of all privileges that you granted on the named table(s) from the users you specify.

■ Use ALTER, DELETE, INSERT, SELECT, or UPDATE as keywords to revoke the use of the corresponding statements. Use the INDEX keyword to revoke the use of the CREATE INDEX statement.

■ Using PUBLIC in the FROM clause removes these privileges from PUBLIC (all users not specifically granted a privilege).

- If you revoke a privilege that you granted using the WITH GRANT OPTION, all users who received that privilege from the designated user (unless they also received that privilege from another user) will lose that privilege.

## Example:

To revoke from user identifiers JOHNDOE and JANEDOE both SELECT and UPDATE access to the table CUSTOMER, enter the following:

```
REVOKE SELECT, UPDATE
  ON CUSTOMER
  FROM JOHNDOE, JANEDOE;
```

## See Also:

GRANT Statement.

# ROLLBACK Statement

## Syntax:

ROLLBACK [WORK]

## Description:

Reverses changes to database tables made since the initiation of the application program, the start of the interactive session, or the last call of the COMMIT statement.

## Notes:

- You can embed this statement in an application program when you precede it with the required EXEC SQL statement prefix and follow it with the SQL statement terminator appropriate to the application language. (See END-EXEC Statement Terminator.)

- The system releases all locks when the ROLLBACK statement is used.

- The system closes all open cursors, destroys any prepared statements, and renders invalid any cursors that you had associated with prepared statements.

- You can use a ROLLBACK statement to reverse any changes made until you execute a COMMIT statement. Note that many data definition commands automatically commit all work done to the point of the execution of the command.

## Example:

In a COBOL program, to reverse all changes made since the last committing statement, enter the following:

```
EXEC SQL
ROLLBACK WORK END-EXEC.
```

In a C program, to reverse all changes made since the last committing statement, enter the following:

```
EXEC SQL
ROLLBACK WORK;
```

## See Also:

COMMIT Statement and LOCK TABLE Statement.

# *Appendixes*

## Common Data Types

| | |
|---|---|
| CHAR[ACTER] (*length*) | A character string with a specified fixed length. |
| VARCHAR (*length*) | A variable-length character string with a specified maximum length. |
| PIC[TURE] *pic-spec* | A display format character string with a picture specification formed according to the rules for the COBOL language. Note that some implementations do not recognize this data type. |
| NUMERIC (*p*[,*q*]) | A number of precision *p* and scale *q*, where *p* is generally less than or equal to 15. Inclusion of the scale is optional. |
| DEC[IMAL] (*p*[,*q*]) | Same as NUMERIC. |
| NUMBER (*p*[,*q*]) | Same as NUMERIC. |
| INTEGER | A binary number, usually in the ranges of −2,147,483,648 through +2,147,483,647 signed, or 0 through 4,294,967,295 unsigned. |
| SMALLINT | A binary number, usually in the ranges of −32,768 through +32,767 signed, or 0 through 65,535 unsigned. Note that some implementations do not make a distinction between INTEGER and SMALLINT. Both are treated as large integers. |
| FLOAT [(*p*)] | A floating point number with precision *p*. |
| REAL | Same as FLOAT, but having implementation-defined precision. |
| DOUBLE PRECISION | Same as REAL. |

# Arithmetic Operators

All implementations support the following arithmetic operators:

| | |
|---|---|
| + ¦ – | Prefix operators. Plus sign (+) does not affect the following expression. Minus sign (–) reverses the sign of the following expression. |
| + | Addition |
| – | Subtraction |
| * | Multiplication |
| / | Division |

Precedence of operations: Expressions within the innermost set of parentheses are evaluated first. Within a set of parentheses, prefix operators are applied before division and multiplication, and division and multiplication are applied before addition and subtraction. When several operations at the same level (such as multiplication and division) appear within a set of parentheses, the operations are performed from left to right.

# Reserved Words

The following is a list of words reserved in the various implementations of SQL. You should not use any of these words to form *column-names*, *table-names*, *view-names*, *correlation-names*, cursor names, *statement-names*, or the names of any other variables in an SQL statement. Consult your product documentation for the specific list of words reserved by your SQL database software.

| | | |
|---|---|---|
| ACCESS | AUDIT | CHARACTER |
| ADD | AUTHORIZATION | CHECK |
| ALL | AVG | CHECKPOINT |
| ALTER | BEGIN | CLEARONPURGE |
| AND | BETWEEN | CLOSE |
| ANY | BREAK | CLUSTER |
| APPEND | BROWSE | CLUSTERED |
| AS | BUFFERPOOL | COBOL |
| ASC | BULK | COLUMN |
| ASCENDING | BY | COMMENT |
| ASSERT | CATALOG | COMMIT |
| ASSIGN | CHAR | COMPRESS |

| | | |
|---|---|---|
| COMPUTE | ERROREXIT | IS |
| CONFIRM | ESCAPE | KEY |
| CONNECT | EVALUATE | KILL |
| CONTAIN | EXCLUSIVE | LANGUAGE |
| CONTAINS | EXEC | LEVEL |
| CONTINUE | EXECUTE | LIKE |
| CONTROLROW | EXISTS | LINENO |
| CONVERT | EXIT | LIST |
| COUNT | FETCH | LOAD |
| CRASH | FIELDPROC | LOCK |
| CREATE | FILE | LOCKSIZE |
| CURRENT | FILLFACTOR | LONG |
| CURSOR | FLOAT | MAX |
| DATABASE | FOR | MAXEXTENTS |
| DATAPAGES | FORMAT | MIN |
| DATE | FORTRAN | MINUS |
| DBA | FOUND | MODE |
| DBCC | FROM | MODIFY |
| DEBUG | GETDEFAULT | MODULE |
| DEC | GO | MOVE |
| DECIMAL | GOTO | NEW |
| DECLARE | GRANT | NOAUDIT |
| DEFAULT | GRAPHIC | NOCOMPRESS |
| DEFINITION | GROUP | NOLIST |
| DELETE | HAVING | NONCLUSTERED |
| DESC | HOLDLOCK | NOSYSSORT |
| DESCENDING | IDENTIFIED | NOT |
| DESCRIPTOR | IF | NOWAIT |
| DISK | IMAGE | NULL |
| DISTINCT | IMMEDIATE | NUMBER |
| DOES | IN | NUMERIC |
| DOUBLE | INCREMENT | NUMPARTS |
| DROP | INDEX | OF |
| DUMMY | INDEXED | OFF |
| DUMP | INDEXPAGES | OFFLINE |
| EACH | INDICATOR | OFFSETS |
| EDITPROC | INITIAL | OLD |
| ELSE | INSERT | ON |
| END | INT | ONCE |
| END-EXEC | INTEGER | ONLINE |
| ERASE | INTERSECT | OPEN |
| ERRLVL | INTO | OPTIMIZE |

OPTION
OR
ORDER
OVER
PART
PARTITION
PASCAL
PCTFREE
PLAN
PLI
PRECISION
PREPARE
PRIMARY
PRINT
PRIOR
PRIQTY
PRIVILEGES
PROC
PROCEDURE
PROCESSEXIT
PUBLIC
RAISERROR
RAW
READTEXT
REAL
RECONFIGURE
RENAME
REPEATABLE
REPLACE
RESOURCE
RETURN
REVOKE
ROLLBACK

ROW
ROWCOUNT
ROWID
ROWNUM
ROWS
RULE
RUN
SAVE
SCHEMA
SECQTY
SECTION
SELECT
SESSION
SET
SETUSER
SHARE
SIZE
SMALLINT
SOME
SPACE
SQL
SQLCODE
SQLERROR
STABLE
START
STATISTICS
STOGROUP
SUCCESSFUL
SUM
SYNONYM
SYSDATE
SYSSORT
TABLE

TABLESPACE
TAPE
TEMPORARY
TEXTSIZE
THEN
TO
TRAN
TRANSACTION
TRIGGER
TRUNCATE
UID
UNION
UNIQUE
UPDATE
USE
USER
USING
VALIDATE
VALIDPROC
VALUES
VARCHAR
VARGRAPHIC
VCAT
VIEW
VOLUMES
WAITFOR
WHENEVER
WHERE
WHILE
WITH
WORK
WRITETEXT

The manuscript for this book was prepared and submitted to Microsoft Press in electronic form. Text files were processed and formatted using Microsoft Word.

Cover design by Thomas A. Draper
Interior text design by Greg Hickman
Principal typography by Rodney Cook

Text composition by Microsoft Press in Times Roman with display in Times Roman Bold, using the Magna composition system and the Linotronic 300 laser imagesetter.

# OTHER TITLES FROM MICROSOFT PRESS

## QUICK REFERENCE GUIDE TO HARD DISK MANAGEMENT

*Van Wolverton*

Don't have time to read a full-length hard disk management book?
Here is all the core information you need to organize, maintain, and
troubleshoot your hard-disk problems along with tips on installing sec-
ondary hard disks, the necessary PC-DOS and MS-DOS commands for
formatting, configuring, and organizing a hard disk, and more.

**72 pages, 4¼ x 11, softcover    $5.95    Order #86-96353**

## IBM® ROM BIOS: PROGRAMMER'S QUICK REFERENCE

*Ray Duncan*

A handy and compact guide to the ROM BIOS services of IBM PC,
PC/AT, and PS/2 machines. The services covered include keyboard,
disk, serial and parallel ports, video display control, memory and
peripheral device configuration information, and access to extended
memory. Duncan provides you with an overview of each ROM BIOS
service along with its required parameters or arguments, its returned
results, and version dependencies.

**128 pages, 4¾ x 8, softcover    $5.95    Order #86-96478**

## MS-DOS® FUNCTIONS: PROGRAMMER'S QUICK REFERENCE

*Ray Duncan*

This useful and functional guide to MS-DOS system service calls includes an overview of each system service (accessed via Interrupts
20H through 2FH). This handy guide also includes the required
parameters or arguments for each function or service, and its returned
results and version dependencies. Duncan also includes special programming notes, uses, and warnings. Covers MS-DOS through
version 3.3.

**128 pages, 4¾ x 8, softcover    $5.95    Order #86-96411**